The Wonder Within You

# the WONDER WITHIN you

celebrating your baby's journey
from conception to birth

CAREY WICKERSHAM

Tyndale House Publishers, Inc.
Carol Stream, Illinois

*The Wonder Within You*

Copyright © 2014 by Carey Wickersham

A Focus on the Family book published by Tyndale House Publishers, Inc., Carol Stream, Illinois 60188.

Focus on the Family and the accompanying logo and design are federally registered trademarks of Focus on the Family, Colorado Springs, CO 80920.

*TYNDALE* and Tyndale's quill logo are registered trademarks of Tyndale House Publishers, Inc.

All Scripture quotations, unless otherwise marked, are taken from the *Holy Bible, New International Version.*® NIV.® Copyright © 1973, 1978, 1984 by Biblica, Inc.® Used by permission of Zondervan. All rights reserved worldwide (www.zondervan.com).

The use of material from or references to various websites does not imply endorsement of those sites in their entirety. Availability of websites and pages is subject to change without notice.

No part of this publication may be reproduced, stored in a retrieval system, or transmitted in any form or by any means—electronic, mechanical, photocopy, recording, or otherwise—without prior written permission of Focus on the Family.

This book is not intended to replace the medical advice of a trained medical professional. Readers are advised to consult a physician or other qualified health-care professional regarding their specific questions or health concerns. The author and publisher specifically disclaim liability, loss, or risk, personal or otherwise, which is incurred as a consequence, directly or indirectly, of the use or application of any of the contents of this book.

Editor: Brandy Bruce
Cover designed by Alberto C. Navata Jr.
Cover photograph copyright © Jamie Grill/Getty Images. All rights reserved.
Interior designed by Jacqueline L. Nuñez.

Sonogram images provided by Jeanette Burlbaw, Prenatal Imaging Centers, Kansas City, Missouri.

Cataloging-in-Publication Data for this book is available by contacting the Library of Congress.

ISBN: 978-1-62405-141-8

Printed in China

20  19  18  17  16  15  14
7   6   5   4   3   2   1

For my twins, Hannah and Hope—
thank you for twenty weeks of pure joy.

# Contents

# Contributors

Seasoned sonographer Jeanette Burlbaw provided all of the ultrasound images for this book, as well as some of the material in the "Development" sections, based on thirty years of peering into the womb. She is a fellow of the Society of Diagnostic Medical Sonography and the American Institute of Ultrasound in Medicine. As a clinical ultrasound educator, she has published cutting-edge research in numerous medical trade journals. She owns and operates Prenatal Imaging Centers in Kansas City, Missouri, and is the mother of two grown children. Additional ultrasound images may be found on the Prenatal Imaging Centers website at www.prenatalimaging.com.

Obstetrician and gynecologist Dr. Kristen Wootton contributed her maternity advice in the "Rx for Health" sections of this book. She is well known for her fabulous bedside manner and tremendous ability to translate complicated medical terminology into information her pregnant patients can easily understand. Wootton is a faculty member at St. Luke's Physician Specialists and an assistant professor at the University of Missouri—Kansas City School of Medicine and Kansas City University of Medicine and Biosciences. Dr. Wootton is also a busy mother of four children.

# Acknowledgments

You know how when you're pregnant, it seems as though delivery day will never come?

Well, I feel like I've been pregnant for about twelve years, because that's how long I've been laboring over this book. Believe me, I didn't conceive, carry, contract, or deliver my "baby" alone. I had loads of help. A doctor and a sonographer, along with midwives, coaches, advisers, tech supporters, back rubbers, dinner makers, tissue holders, intercessors, nurses, friends, organizers, marketers, mamas, and miracle makers all walked in and out of my life during my baby's decade-long gestation. Most of them helped me for one reason alone: they want moms to know how amazing their babies are so they can better nurture new life.

So thank you, Hope and Hannah. You are forever in my heart. If it weren't for you, I wouldn't have taken the first steps to research the beginning of life. This is your legacy to the world.

Marty, Abby, and Daniel—you are my greatest loves and my best teachers, the reasons I get up in the morning and fall into bed exhausted at night. I'm so glad you are mine.

Dad, you have believed in and supported me from day one. Your sweet pea is forever in your debt.

Mom, thank you for dreaming with me and raising me to love babies. I hope your vision for this book comes true, and that you witness it happening from heaven.

To Mandy and Jenny and Heidi and Kathy and Irene—I'm glad we're on this journey together. You make it so much richer.

Jeanette Burlbaw—I remember the day I met you. You introduced me to my boy in 3-D, and it changed my life. How could you have stuck with me for so long? You and your magic wand inspire me and thousands of other moms . . . daily. Thank you from all of us.

Dr. Kristen Wootton—not many women get to have their friend deliver their baby. But that's probably how all your patients feel. Thank you for having the best bedside manner ever and for teaching your residents to have the same respect for women that you have.

Jill, you make what I do look so much prettier. You shine it up with graphics and video and organization until it sparkles. In a pinch, you're the one I run to and learn from and laugh with, and if all else fails, we just yell, "Galen!"

Thanks to the patients at Prenatal Imaging Centers in Kansas City who gladly shared their stories and baby images with me. And thank you, Lisa, for helping me get all those consents!

Thanks to Dr. Dan Gehlbach, Nicolas Rodriguez, and Sheryl May from Midwest Reproductive Center for the information and images of baby in weeks two and three.

Thank you, Wade Sisson, for the hours you spent designing my website. Your friendship and expertise bolstered a lot more than my SEO!

To Cathy Gordon and the midwives and mamas at New Birth Company—thanks for being quick on the draw whenever I needed help or advice. You girls rock the cradles and rule the world!

Thank you to Jeanette and Mark Littleton and the writers at the

Heart of America Christian Writers' Network (HACWN). Your conferences taught me the basics of book writing and encouraged me along the way.

To my editor in shining armor, Brandy Bruce. If I had half the organizational skills you do, I could whip a thousand repetitive redundancies with one sword tied behind my back. I obviously don't. Thankfully, you slayed a lot of those fire breathers for me.

Thank you to Larry Weeden and Allison Montjoy at Focus on the Family. You believed, let me dream big and vent, and carried on with the message.

To Linda, Nancy, Jackie, and Stephen at Tyndale House—you guys got in my canoe when I was paddling upstream and installed a 250-horsepower engine. I'm so thankful, as my arms were really tired! You are a great team!

To my tried and true agent, Les Stobbe. Did ya know when you signed me that I would be *this* much trouble? Thanks for your advice and for helping me fight. I always knew if my passion got me in trouble, you'd just come in with a bucket and bail me out.

To my mama-friends and their mama-friends, who had their babies imaged and responded to my pleas for stories and took me to tea and listened and prayed and asked and cared and shared my questions and dug up answers . . . thank you. As mothers, you all pitched in to help me get 'er done. Without you, I couldn't have. So here's to you and all your babies!

To God, who brought triumph out of tragedy. May these words of my mouth and this meditation of my heart be pleasing in Your sight, Lord, my Rock and my Redeemer.

# Preface

*My dear Mama-friend,*

*Two tiny lines inside a window on a six-inch piece of plastic. It's the universal sign of "my life will never be the same."*

*Congratulations! Whether you planned it or not, you're pregnant, and you are now a card-carrying member of a history-spanning club of women that is more than a millennium in the making.*

*Black, white, brown, Protestant, Catholic, Jewish, Muslim, Republican, Democrat, sixteen, or sixty-seven—we're all in this together. And be glad, because we need one another. For laughs, for advice, for information, for encouragement, and for hand-me-down maternity clothes!*

*Within the pages of this book, hundreds of women shared their stories . . . for you. Some stories you'll relate to; others I hope you don't. But motherhood pushes all our differences aside and brings us together. The earth's baby growers have a common bond. The circle is meant to be forever widened. You are warmly invited to clasp new hands in this rich season of life. So let me be among the many to extend my arms in welcome. I'm smiling with you.*

*Our mothers and their mothers never had a pregnancy book like this. In the past two decades, the widespread advances of the ultrasound have changed everything. We* can see what our female predecessors could only imagine, and a picture is worth a thousand decades of maternal musings.

During a healthy pregnancy, most of us get only a few peeks at our unborn babes. The Wonder Within You *lets you peer through a womb window every week. You can watch as baby grows and changes. You can see the differences in baby's moods and appearances. These are distinctions DNA set in motion from day one.*

*GE's new HDlive ultrasound technology is amazing. Because of it, we're able to study baby's facial expressions, personality, and preferences. Studies show these images help us bond to our babies and empower us to make better prenatal decisions. The images are so clear, they often look like photographs, but they're captured with sound waves. Because of the way the waves bounce inside the uterus, it may appear that parts of baby that aren't "in focus," so to speak, are missing. Rest assured, baby is intact.*

*Throughout the book, you'll notice the Play button next to the ultrasound photos. If you scan the QR code (quick-response barcode) above it with your smartphone, you'll be able to watch a very short ultrasound video clip. If you don't have a smartphone, borrow one (or access the site via the URL) so you can take advantage of this unique feature of the book. Watching these little ones move is amazing!*

*I hope you relish the videos, the ultrasound images of baby, and the stories from moms as much as I did when*

*I included them. Use this book to journal your pregnancy moments and record your milestones. Someday you may want to give it to your child as a keepsake. Because who knows what pregnancy will be like for our babies' babies?*

*Your friend,*

*Carey*

*PS: Join me at www.thewonderwithinyou.com for more stories, images, and information! I would love to hear from you as well. To me, there is nothing richer than a good baby story.*

# week ONE

Your future houseguest is calling in a womb reservation

# week ONE

## GETTING READY

Your ovaries release an egg or two (or sometimes more) each month, usually around the fourteenth day of your menstrual cycle. The egg emerges from an ovary and travels down the fallopian tube, where it can meet sperm to start a process called fertilization. Health-care providers begin the countdown to your baby's grand entrance on the first day of your last missed period. That's two weeks before the tiniest form of baby even exists. For now, it's as if your future houseguest is calling in a womb reservation two weeks out.

When your egg actually joins with a sperm at the end of week two, it's baby time! The average pregnancy lasts approximately forty weeks from that day. For women who don't conceive in a given cycle, the lining of the uterus (called the endometrium) is shed during the menstrual period. The endometrium then thickens again in preparation for receiving a fertilized egg in the next menstrual cycle.

*Making the decision to have a child is momentous. It is to decide forever to have your heart go walking around outside your body.*
—ELIZABETH STONE, AUTHOR

# Rx for Health

Women who are considering pregnancy should see a health-care provider prior to conception for a complete physical exam. Your provider can offer suggestions for optimizing the timing of conception and may recommend possible preconception testing options. At the appointment, individual concerns and risks can be addressed. Your provider will also likely recommend or prescribe a prenatal vitamin for you to take even before you conceive.

You and your partner should stop smoking, drinking alcohol, and taking any medications that aren't allowed during pregnancy. Illicit drugs are especially harmful to a developing baby.

**NUTRITIONAL NUGGET**
Proper nutrition is important before and after you conceive. Your body will function optimally (as will your reproductive system) when you eat a healthy, balanced diet. Eat your fruits and veggies, avoid trans fats, and select complex carbohydrates in favor of simple carbohydrates and refined sugars. If you're trying to conceive, try to get to your optimal weight now. Being extremely over- or underweight often affects your menstrual cycle and can prevent regular ovulation.

## MOMMY MOMENTS

### "I Always Knew"

Some women dream of being a mother from a very early age. Some decide much later. For others, it's not a conscious decision; it's a total surprise.

*I knew I wanted to have a baby even when I was a little girl and loved dolls.* —CAROL SUE WICKERSHAM

*I started noticing all the strollers at the mall. They had always been there; I was just taking notice of them.* —CELESTE KIRMER

*I knew I wanted to have another one when I started to dream about babies in my sleep.* —SARA LISSAUER

*We had been married for several years and I was giving my dog, Willy, birthday parties with hot dogs and cake! It was time.* —TRACY MCMINN

*It was like something turned on inside of me, and once it was turned on, I couldn't turn it off. Everywhere I looked I'd see babies galore, and even my husband was noticing every couple with a baby. We were ready.* —BECCA CLARK

*I always wanted to be a mom, but there were unexpected delays in getting there. I came to a point where I thought I might never have the privilege. But God's plan for me was best. My daughter, Charley, and son, Nash, are gifts that were sent at just the perfect time.* —STACIA WINKLER

# PRENATAL POSTCARD

## The Trials of Waiting by Tess Koppelman

This is it. This is going to be the month. I can feel it. My boobs hurt, I'm feeling strange, maybe a little overly emotional, and I'm really, really tired. Then there's the crinkle of the plastic wrap, a pee test, a two-minute wait, and then . . . a big . . . fat . . . negative.

That's the routine every month. Every month is filled with excitement, thinking about what could be. Then there's the disappointment. It wasn't meant to be. Pick yourself up, try not to be upset, and try and try again.

I didn't think it would be this way. Even though I'm thirty-six, I'm pretty healthy, and the doctor says everything looks fine. So what's the problem? Am I doing something wrong? Do I want it too much? Do I not want it enough? Am I overthinking it and stressing myself out, thereby sabotaging everything? Or is it really this hard to have a baby? Then why does it seem like some couples get pregnant just by sipping out of the same glass?

Maybe I waited too long. I spent the majority of my adult life focused on my career. I didn't even think I wanted a child. The idea of having someone dependent on me practically gave me hives. But then you grow up a little. You see your friends having kids and think, Hey, this little being isn't so scary. I could do that.

Just three months after my husband and I started "trying," I did have that one positive. But it turned out to be an ectopic pregnancy. An overly eager sperm found its way to the egg but attached to my ovary instead of landing in my uterus. Trust me, that's not a good thing. It involved lots of medical stuff and staff who are now familiar with every inch of my reproductive organs.

So we'll keep trying. And maybe next month will be that big fat positive. I hope.

# ONLY A DREAM

*Remember when you were a little girl, and you first thought of me? Did you hold your dolls and pretend they breathed and laughed and cried? I'm going to make your baby dreams come true. Only better. I will love you back. I'll trust you completely. My cheeks will warm to your kisses.*

*Someday I'll smile at you and run to the door with my arms in the air when you come in. I might cry sometimes too. Right now I'm still a dream, but I'm about to make a lifetime of your dreams come true.*

## BABY NOTES

Describe your earliest thoughts about becoming a mother.

........................................................................................................

........................................................................................................

........................................................................................................

........................................................................................................

........................................................................................................

........................................................................................................

........................................................................................................

........................................................................................................

........................................................................................................

# week
## TWO

Start consuming a healthful diet now
(even if you're not pregnant yet!)

# week TWO

## FERTILIZATION

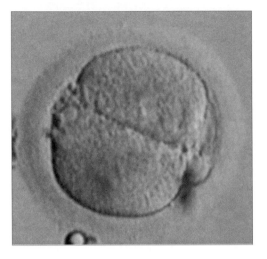

www.tyndal.es/twwyweek2

(Photo by Dan Gehlbach, Midwest Reproductive Center, Olathe, KS)

At the end of week two, twenty-four hours after fertilization, one cell becomes two as the journey to birth begins. This tiny, two-cell embryo is magnified about three hundred times. The sperm fertilized the egg in the fallopian tube less than twenty-four hours ago, usually about fourteen days after the first day of your last period. In the next few days, this fertilized egg will multiply many more times. Next stop: your uterus, about six days after fertilization. The genetic code for your baby, including hair and eye color and even some personality traits, are all wrapped up in this microscopic group of cells.

# Development

One of the thousands of eggs you were born with is ripening and almost ready to be released. At the end of this week (about day fourteen of a normal twenty-eight-day menstrual cycle), you will probably ovulate. That happens when a hormonal surge causes the egg to leave the ovary. This is the optimal time to get pregnant. Increased mucus in the vaginal wall at this time helps the sperm makes its journey to the egg.

During intercourse, two hundred million to six hundred million sperm are deposited in the vagina. They swim through the cervix, the opening to the uterus, and move through the uterus toward the egg or eggs that are in the fallopian tubes. Your egg contains half the DNA needed for a new baby. The sperm contains the other half and ultimately determines the sex of the baby. Each egg allows only one sperm to fertilize it. Immediately after the first sperm penetrates the wall of the egg, the wall closes so that no additional sperm can enter. In the case of twins, there are either two eggs with two fertilizing sperm, resulting in fraternal twins, or one egg and one sperm that divide later, resulting in identical twins.

# Rx for Health

Your prenatal vitamin should contain enough folic acid to meet your daily requirement. For women who have already had a child with a neural-tube defect, the US Public Health Service recommends 4,000 mcg (4 mg) of folic acid.[1]

**NUTRITIONAL NUGGET**
If you want a healthy baby, start consuming a healthful diet now (even if you're not pregnant yet!). That includes getting at least 400 micrograms (mcg) of folic acid before you get pregnant, and 600 mcg once you are pregnant.[2] Folic acid helps prevent neural-tube defects that often occur in a developing baby even before a woman realizes she is pregnant.[3] It also promotes the growth of the baby's tissues and organs. Breakfast cereal is often fortified with folic acid. Natural sources of folic acid include dark-green, leafy vegetables, strawberries, bananas, milk, oranges, peanuts, almonds, whole grains, and dried beans. Refined grain products like bread and pasta also contain folic acid.

# MOMMY MOMENTS

## Prep Work

If your pregnancy is planned, you're probably laying some foundations mentally, financially, and even physically for becoming a mother. Here are some of the first steps moms-to-be often take:

*I read lots of baby books. I think some doctors assume moms today know so much, but there were lots of things I had no idea I was supposed to do or not do during pregnancy. The books helped me feel more confident.*
—KATHY HAIVALA

*I took a bigger interest in what I was eating and what I should most definitely avoid. For example, I read more food labels to see if there were any artificial sweeteners or high levels of sodium. I didn't want to consume a lot of these items.* —HEATHER ENGLAND

*I had to quit smoking, which was easier because I knew that there was a baby growing inside me. I also started exercising more. I felt I had to be in better shape to withstand the demands of a pregnancy.* —KARLA SHOTTS

*When I was pregnant with number two, I would point out other siblings to my son that we would see being helpful or kind. I would mention to him that he would be helping his brother or sister soon too. For example, we would see a baby crying in the grocery store, and then see a big brother or sister comforting the baby. I would tell my son that he would get to do sweet things like that!*
—STEPHANIE HARROW

# PRENATAL POSTCARD

## Plan B by Luna Leverette

I had a plan. Two boys, three years apart. Done by the age of thirty. For two years, my husband and I tried everything to conceive. One month, just after ovulation, I thought we had it right. I was wrong. Between Mother's Day and Memorial Day, I took weekly pregnancy tests. Negative. Negative. And negative.

Frustrated by months of failed attempts, my husband and I had "the talk." We agreed to allow doctors to check us but decided that we didn't want to use medical intervention to get pregnant. If it didn't happen naturally, we would accept it and spend baby money on a trip to Europe.

The next day, I took another test. Two lines appeared. The second was faint and fuzzy. Dazed, I walked down the hall holding the test. I softly said, "What does this mean?" My husband and I sat there at the kitchen table staring at the stick. The next morning, I took another test. Two strong lines! I was so very happy. It got even better when the ultrasound showed I was having the first boy in my family in sixty years.

After Andy was born, we planned to wait a while before trying for baby number two. But just after my son's first birthday, surprise! A pregnancy test produced two strong lines!

For some reason, I just knew this baby was a girl. I was fearful of having a daughter because I didn't have a good relationship with my mom. When the ultrasound showed we were having a girl, I just said, "I know!" Our daughter, Keira, was born twenty-one months and one day after Andy. And despite my initial worries, I couldn't imagine the world without her.

In less than two years, I had two beautiful, healthy children. Not by the age of thirty, not three years apart, and not two boys. That was my plan, but this was God's. And I've found that His is so much better.

# GET READY

*I'm about to change your life. Rock your world. Make you scream and cry or jump up and down and dance. Nothing will be the same after I come. Some things will be worse, but most will be better. I'll fill your life with joy. Laughter. Love. Questions. Happiness and stress. I'll fill you up, and I'll probably let you down sometimes. But I will change you. Now. Forever.*

*So get ready. Here I come!*

## BABY NOTES

Where were you when you found out you were pregnant? How did you react?

....................................................................................................

....................................................................................................

....................................................................................................

....................................................................................................

....................................................................................................

....................................................................................................

....................................................................................................

....................................................................................................

....................................................................................................

# week
# THREE

Your baby has his or her own
genetic code

# week THREE

## DIVIDE AND CONQUER

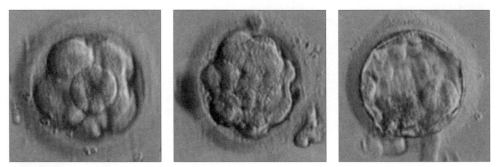

www.tyndal.es/twwyweek3

This week is one of phenomenal growth. Baby's cells are rapidly dividing. In the first image, you see an eight-cell division. The second image is the morula, a group of sixteen cells formed by day four. Five days after fertilization, baby is called a blastocyst, made up of about one hundred cells. In the last image, the cells around the edges are the future placenta. The cells gathered at the bottom of the circle make up the blastocyst. In the middle, there is a tiny bit of amniotic fluid swirling. If your baby was conceived naturally, he or she will float down your fallopian tube and implant in the wall of your uterus. If fertilization occurred under a microscope, as with in vitro fertilization, the doctor will transfer the cells to your uterus at the end of this week.

# Development

I start out as only two cells on a mission, but I'm dividing and multiplying fast. I have my own unique genetic code. My hair and eye color and thousands of other things about the way I'll be are already determined. If the fertilizing sperm contributed a Y chromosome, I'm a boy. If the sperm contributed an X chromosome, I'm a girl. I'm starting to produce lots of extra hormones in you even though I'm only the size of the period at the end of this sentence.

# Rx for Health

Approximately three to four days after fertilization, the morula (the fertilized egg after multiple cell division) enters the uterus. By the end of this week, the blastocyst (preembryo) implants in the lining of the uterus. Most women won't know they've conceived yet; however, some may experience a small amount of vaginal bleeding with implantation. If this is confused with the start of your period, it can throw off your due date.

It's important to contact your health-care provider if you have any vaginal bleeding, because even though it might be normal, it could also be a sign of a miscarriage or an ectopic pregnancy. Your provider might want to do some blood work to measure the pregnancy hormone level as well as confirm your blood type.

**NUTRITIONAL NUGGET**
Pregnant women need more protein (during the second half of pregnancy), more folic acid, and more iron than do nonpregnant women.[1] Pregnant women over the age of eighteen need the same amount of calcium—1,000 mg/day—as their nonpregnant counterparts.[2] Getting those nutrients takes a concerted effort. Based on nutritional guidelines, here is a list of recommended servings per day from each food group to help you keep track:[3]

- Bread and cereal: 6–11 servings
- Vegetables: 3–5 servings
- Fruit: 2–4 servings
- High-calcium foods: 3 servings
- Meat or meat substitutes: 2–4 (3–4 oz.) servings

# Mommy Moments

## Mixed Feelings

It's one of the most important decisions you'll ever make. To be or not to be . . . a mother? That is the question that usually triggers a barrage of intense emotion.

*I worried most about two things: Will he be healthy, and can we really do this?* —Laurisa Myers

*I was most excited about a new life in our home.* —Ailene Banks

*When I found out I was pregnant, I cried—a combination of being happy and scared.* —Irene Haivala

*I had to prepare emotionally at the thought of becoming a mother. I was shocked to find out I was pregnant, and I didn't think I was ready.* —Becky Morrell

*My husband wanted to wait until we had been married two years to have a baby. He called it his "no compete clause." When it expired, I was ready! But I was slightly worried about finances.* —Lynne Carols

*We found out we were having twins. I was completely overwhelmed. My husband was ecstatic.* —Marianne Hering

# PRENATAL POSTCARD

## Pregnant on the Pill by Melissa Bellach

We wanted children. But I never dreamed I would be holding our five-day-old baby on our first wedding anniversary. Impossible! I was on the pill. Three months after our wedding, we took a beach trip with family. When we got home, we joked about my late period. The next week, during my lunch break, I took a pregnancy test in the bathroom of the drugstore. I was sure it would read negative. I was wrong. That one moment was the most intense of my life. "I'm going to be a mom?" I kept repeating.

On the way back to work, I was shaking and crying uncontrollably. I wasn't sad, just emotional. I called my husband from the car. He was off work and standing in an aisle at Home Depot.

"You know how we've been joking about me being pregnant?" I said.

"Yes," he said.

"Well, it isn't a joke. I am."

We were both quiet. Then he started laughing . . . hysterical, happy laughter.

I cried in my office most of the afternoon. When I called my mom, bewildered tears were still falling. As I told her, the words "I'm pregnant" rang in my ears. I felt like I was moving under-water. And then I heard her start to laugh too! Like it was the most wonderful shock ever. I came home exhausted but calmer. When my husband hugged me, it began to sink in, and we celebrated. The baby's due date was supposed to be on our one-year anniversary. But, of course, our very deter-mined healthy baby boy once again surprised us and arrived a little earlier than planned.

# A SECRET

*Even though I'm really small, just a group of growing cells, I have a secret. It's a biggie. For now it's classified. My little lips are zipped. You're choosing names and wondering whether I'm a boy or girl. But only God knows. And He's not telling yet. Hush-hush. Until we want you to know, you'll have to wait. But not for long. After all, I'm just bursting to tell you so you can tell everyone else our secret.*

## BABY NOTES

Whom are you sharing this journey with? Whom do you tell your secrets about life, your dreams, your fears, and your hopes?

....................................................................

....................................................................

....................................................................

....................................................................

....................................................................

....................................................................

....................................................................

....................................................................

....................................................................

# week FOUR

Each one of your baby's
cells is different

# week FOUR

## I'm This Big: I'm .04 of an inch long.[1]

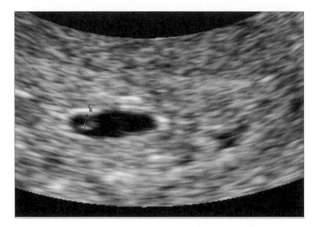

www.tyndal.es/twwyweek4

Even when three- or four-dimensional images are available, sonographers usually prefer 2-D pictures at this early stage of development. In this image, you see what look like two sacs: a large one in the middle and a much smaller spot lower and to the right. But there is just one baby. The dark spot on the right is where blood vessels have broken during the baby's implantation. Within the sac on the left, you can see a little circle. This is the yolk sac, which provides the baby's nutrition before the placenta develops. This image of baby was taken vaginally early in the fourth week. The heart will start to beat in just a few days.

*Life is always a rich and steady time when you are waiting for something to happen or to hatch.*
—E. B. White,
*Charlotte's Web*

# DEVELOPMENT

When I arrive in the uterus, I start digging into the lining of your uterine wall. This process can take four to six days. I start to draw nutrients from your blood supply, and my spinal cord begins to develop. The amniotic cavity where I will live for the next nine months is taking shape. The yolk sac forms next to the fertilized egg. This is how I get nutrition until the placenta is more fully developed. Each one of my cells is different. I'm called an embryo now, which in Greek means "growing within."

# RX FOR HEALTH

At this point, most women don't know they are pregnant. Estrogen, progesterone, and HCG (human chorionic gonadotropin) are hormones that surge immediately after the fertilized egg implants in the uterus. Some mothers experience nausea and vomiting as early as the end of the fifth week, brought on by the hormone spike.

In the rare case that the mother loses more than 10 percent of her body weight because of vomiting or dehydration, she is often hospitalized and given proper nutrition. The baby takes the nutrients needed for development from Mom and is rarely harmed.

At the end of this week, the hormone HCG, excreted in a pregnant mother's urine, is probably high enough to be detected by a home pregnancy test (HPT). A blood test at a doctor's office can determine pregnancy as early as twenty-four to forty-eight hours after implantation. A vaginal sonogram can confirm pregnancy by four to five weeks.

**NUTRITIONAL NUGGET**
Calcium is an important nutrient for the baby's bone development. The baby draws calcium from your blood supply. If you don't have enough there, it will come from your bones. If this happens, the risk of osteoporosis may increase later in life. During pregnancy, a lack of calcium may also increase sleeplessness, muscle cramps, and blood pressure. Try to get between 1,000 and 1,300 milligrams (mg) of calcium every day.[2] That means roughly four to five servings of milk; cheese; yogurt; green, leafy vegetables; or salmon a day. Many prenatal vitamins don't offer this much calcium, so it's important to incorporate calcium into your diet.

# MOMMY MOMENTS
## Mother's Intuition

*Emotionally excruciating.* Two words that describe the two weeks before it's possible to get two lines on a home pregnancy test. Most home tests aren't accurate until after the first missed day of your period. That's about fourteen days after you ovulate and possibly conceive. Before that, if you're pregnant, your hormones know it even if your head doesn't. And your heart is likely whipping your emotions into a frothed latte of frenzy. Still, some women have their first nudge of mother's intuition before the test proves it's valid.

*I've never been afraid of heights, but before I knew I was pregnant with my first, I hiked up Seven Falls while on vacation in Colorado Springs. I was dizzy and terrified when I looked over the edge. I knew right then I was pregnant! A test later that day confirmed it.* —Karla Shotts

*During my second pregnancy, in 1985, I had an inkling. First, some pain in my lower abdomen, and then a feeling in my heart. The nagging hunch was strong enough that I bought a pregnancy test even before I missed my period. It was positive. I went straight to the doctor, where the test came back . . . negative. Another month went by with no period, so I returned to the doctor. This time the test confirmed what my intuition told me almost a month earlier.* —Betty Ost-Everley

*It was too soon to take a test, but I had been pregnant three times before and just knew I would soon have number four. I was so sure that I started writing a letter to a daughter. Several weeks later my intuition was proven right. Nine months later I delivered a healthy, precious girl.* —Sheila Howe

# Prenatal Postcard

## A Stowaway in Colorado
## by Michelle Smith

After more than four years of marriage, my husband and I had warmed up to the idea of having a baby. But just a few weeks after deciding we were open to the notion of parenthood, I felt that maybe it wasn't the right time. I was in a period of transition with my career. So while on a vacation out in Colorado to see some friends, my husband and I talked it over and decided to wait a while longer before trying again for a baby.

We spent our vacation trekking over Colorado—steaming in hot springs, rambling in a Jeep up the side of a mountain (and nearly tipping over), white-water rafting, and kayaking. While at a restaurant in Crested Butte, Colorado, after a full day of fun, I'd cleaned my plate of food, and the others at the table joked that I must be pregnant. We all laughed, but I certainly didn't think it was true. To my thinking, it was a good thing I wasn't pregnant! Not with all my adventures, like rafting down the river!

After we returned home to Texas, I noticed that my Colorado appetite hadn't changed. I was still eating way more than usual. This change in my appetite caused me to wonder if maybe I really was pregnant. I hadn't missed my period, but I had a feeling something was going on inside me. So I bought a test and saw those little pink lines surface.

My husband was in the yard. I walked outside, holding the test in my hand.

"What's that?" he asked me.

"I'm pregnant," I told him.

He was thrilled and hugged me. Ready or not, our baby, Gillian, was snug inside me. We didn't know it then, but she'd make her grand entrance nearly nine weeks ahead of schedule. She's fearless and strong. I'm not surprised. After all, she was riding rapids before she was born.

## "I'M ATTACHED TO YOU"

*A connection that will endure for generations has just been formed. A new beginning. On this journey of life, we are now eternally attached. You and me. The bond grows stronger every day. I'm trying to let you know that you have a new life growing inside of you. VIP—that's me. I'm here right now. As monumental as a fresh day. As tiny as the start of a wish. We are unaware of the new direction your life will travel because of mine, but let's clasp hands and explore. You are my first partner and friend. My best protector and teacher. Together, let's embark on the unknown adventure that awaits you and me.*

## BABY NOTES

Did you have any idea you were pregnant before you had a positive pregnancy test?

..................................................................................

..................................................................................

..................................................................................

..................................................................................

..................................................................................

..................................................................................

..................................................................................

..................................................................................

# week FIVE

The biggest part of the baby is now the heart

# week FIVE

### I'M THIS BIG: I'm one-eighth of an inch long.

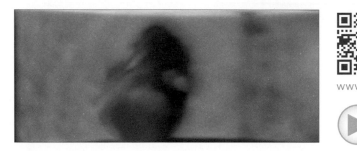

www.tyndal.es/twwyweek5

*Every good and perfect gift is from above.*
—JAMES 1:17

This is a very rare look at baby in 3-D. This early in gestation, sonographers usually aren't asked to image with 3-D technology. In this sonogram, you see the mother's uterus surrounding the tiny baby. Inside the sac, on the right side, is the developing embryo. The biggest part of baby is now the heart. The heart rate fluctuates greatly at this point. It may beat up to 175 times a minute.[1] By the twentieth week of pregnancy, the heart has matured and pumps blood more efficiently at 120 to 160 beats per minute.[2] Often, a sonographer can tell by the fifth week if the mother is having more than one baby.

# Development

By week five, my presence in your uterus causes you to miss your menstrual period. The cells in my brain are forming. Although I'm tiny, I'm big enough to be seen via sonogram. My little heart parts are beginning to form and beat. A sonogram can often detect the quick rhythm of my heart. My central nervous system, muscles, bones, and skeleton, and most of my major systems form during my first eight weeks of life. There is a tiny amount of fluid in my amniotic sac. I have (or rather, the placenta has) produced enough hormones that a home pregnancy test should now read positive.

# Rx for Health

The first trimester in the womb represents the most rapid growth rate in a person's entire life. Remarkable changes occur daily as cells divide and future organ systems form. There are so many things happening that the possibility for error exists. This is when folic acid supplementation and avoidance of certain medications are critical. Schedule an appointment as soon as you get a positive home pregnancy test, especially if you have a history of miscarriages. Your health-care provider may recommend hormones or blood thinners. If you're unsure of when your last menstrual period was, the doctor may schedule a sonogram to determine the age of your baby.

**NUTRITIONAL NUGGET**
Zinc is especially important now and throughout your pregnancy because it helps with healthy cell division and growth. Later it may prevent premature delivery and aid in the healing process. Some women have zinc deficiencies, which have been linked to preterm labor.[3] Get approximately 10 mg or more of zinc per day from food sources like meat, whole grains, nuts, beets, and carrots.[4]

# MOMMY MOMENTS

## "I'm What!?"

Pregnancy. In a single moment, it expands the definition of you as a woman to you as a mother. In an unforgettable nanosecond, everything inside you blurs as you take in the announcement of new life. Ask any mother from sixteen to ninety-six, and she will remember the moment she knew that one person had become two.

*The day I found out I was pregnant, I was afraid to sit down in case such extreme movement would hurt my baby.* —SUZANNE FIELD

*When I found out I was pregnant, I couldn't believe my eyes! We had tried for six years, so to get a positive result on a pregnancy test was unbelievable.* —SUSAN GIMOTTY

*I called the doctor that day and made an appointment, and then I spent the next week online researching the accuracy of pregnancy tests!* —TRICIA CAMBRON

*When I found out I was pregnant, I danced around outside in my bathrobe waving the pregnancy test and shouting, "We got two lines!" Then I called everybody to tell them!* —AMANDA CHAPMAN

# PRENATAL POSTCARD

## A Sign from Above by Jacque Wilson

My husband, Mark, and I discovered I was pregnant with our second child just before Valentine's Day. We felt excited, thankful, and nervous. An early sonogram revealed our little "grain of rice" floating comfortably in my uterus. Everything was fine. We made Valentine's cards to announce our pregnancy. When we photocopied the image, we got our own surprise. There was a faint but distinct shadow of a heart surrounding our precious baby. The sense of peace we desperately needed washed over us.

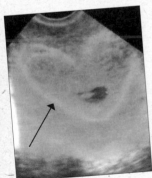

You see, Mark and I lost our first baby, Ryan, to a heart defect. He was only six months old. Deciding to have another baby was difficult. We grieved for two years before we were ready to try again. Then we battled fear. The image of the heart that surrounded our baby girl was a sign from God for us. It was as if He was telling us it was going to be okay.

The heart image around baby Sadie was explained scientifically as a reflection of sound waves off the uterine wall. Out of the thousands of angles possible, our sonographer unwittingly chose this one. We know it wasn't an accident.

Sadie is a tremendous blessing to us. She knows all about her brother, Ryan, who lives in heaven. My husband and I are now expecting our third child. Sadie says it's a girl. She says she already has a brother. She's right; she does.

# SURPRISE!

*Get up! I've been trying to tell you. Trying to show you all the early signs. It's time you figured out the big surprise. I've been cooking this up for a pretty long time. I think you might suspect I'm alive. So let's go! Get a test. I need some attention down here. More food. More rest. Less stress. Take that test!*

*Yippee! Did you see? I told you. It was me. I was making you feel all squishy inside. Now let's go tell everybody our big surprise!*

## BABY NOTES

How did you break the exciting news to family and friends that a baby was on the way? Whom did you tell first?

........................................................................

........................................................................

........................................................................

........................................................................

........................................................................

........................................................................

........................................................................

........................................................................

# week SIX

Your baby's single-chambered
heart is beating

# week SIX

*A person's a person,
no matter how small.*
—DR. SEUSS,
*Horton Hears a Who!*

## I'M THIS BIG: I'm one-quarter of an inch long.

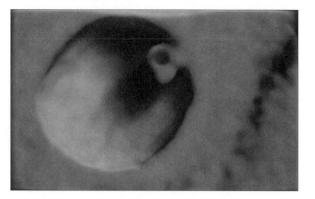

www.tyndal.es/twwyweek6

A sonographer can probably see your baby's heartbeat if you have a vaginal sonogram at this point in your pregnancy. In this image, you can see baby tucked in the womb connected to the yolk sac. The yolk sac is the circle on the right. Baby is in the shape of a C, attached to the yolk sac along the bottom left, just underneath the sac.

# Development

My single-chambered heart begins beating three weeks and one day after fertilization. Blood cells are circulating inside me. My chest, head, and abdomen are taking shape. Buds are forming that will soon be my arms and legs. My eyes, ears, and mouth are developing. My lungs, liver, and stomach are intact. Amniotic fluid surrounds and protects me. I'm about the size of a lentil bean. I'm growing about one-tenth of a centimeter every day.

# Rx for Health

The cardiovascular system is the first system of an embryo to function. The heart begins to beat at the beginning of the sixth week from the first day of the last menstrual period (or four weeks from fertilization). The average heart rate is between 120 and 160 beats per minute but may be as low as 90 or as high as 180 beats per minute. Most heart defects are multifactorial in nature. Women with a personal or family history of congenital heart defects may want to seek genetic counseling prior to conceiving to understand the risks.

**NUTRITIONAL NUGGET**
You should be eating at least one serving of vitamin A–rich foods a day. Usually these are dark green or bright orange in color. They help with cell growth and development of healthy skin, bones, and eyes. Vitamin A may also help your body fight infection. Foods rich in vitamin A include sweet potatoes, carrots, kale, apricots, cantaloupe, strawberries, tomatoes, whole milk, egg yolks, and cod.

Too much vitamin A can harm the baby. Pregnant women eighteen years of age or younger should get at least 750 micrograms per day but not more than 2,800 mcg; pregnant women older than eighteen should receive at least 770 mcg daily but not more than 3,000.[1]

## Mommy Moments

### Hearing and Seeing Your Baby's Heartbeat

If you're more than six weeks along and you have a sonogram, you'll probably see a little blink on the screen and hear a pulsing sound. That's your baby's heartbeat. Seeing your little one's heart beating for the first time is an unforgettable experience. How can something so minuscule elicit such emotion?

*The moment we heard the baby's heartbeat, my husband stood straight up from his chair. He walked up to the screen, where we could see a flickering heartbeat, and stood there in amazement.* —Brandy Bruce

*I didn't know what to expect the first time the doctor was listening for the heartbeat, but when the sound of it was clear, I unexpectedly broke into giggles. I could hardly stop laughing long enough for the doctor to finish listening!* —Tricia Cambron

*I was overwhelmed with the reality of it all. Until then, I was just counting on the accuracy of the pregnancy test. The heartbeat made it real for me.* —Kathy Haivala

*Because of my hormone levels, I suspected I might be carrying twins. At eight weeks, we had our first sonogram, and I saw the image of two sacs, each with a heartbeat. I started crying. It was so surreal seeing their images on the screen.* —Kara Broeker

# PRENATAL POSTCARD

## The Will to Survive by Serenity Bohon

Three weeks after my positive pregnancy test, I was diagnosed with cancer. I was so scared, I could barely breathe. The lump on my shoulder had been there for a while. It hurt, but we hoped it was a cyst. Instead, it was a malignant tumor.

My oncologist recommended surgery to cure the synovial cell sarcoma. The anesthesiologist felt the baby was at risk, but my surgeon persisted. If the cancer spread to my lungs, there was little chance my baby or I would live until delivery. I was thirteen weeks pregnant on the day of surgery. Our best hope was to remove the cancer immediately at its original site.

I wondered if it was possible that my child could endure my illness. How could an unborn baby fight a disease that even I struggled to find the strength to fight?

The most wonderful sound in the world was my baby's heartbeat after surgery. I finally felt hope that we might both survive.

Several weeks later, in an ultrasound my baby raised his arm with a clenched fist held high. It was like a message to me. He was stronger than I had imagined.

The surgery was successful; my physicians didn't recommend chemotherapy. They planned radiation for after the baby was born. It was hard to believe my womb was safe enough for the baby. Yet he remained there without a single complication. When he finally arrived, screaming mad and overwhelmed by the shock of a strange and cold environment, I felt intensely connected to him. We had been through so much together. That night I held him close, awestruck that life thrived in turmoil . . . and inspired like never before at the miracle.

Jake taught me about strength—the strength of life itself, and how difficult it is to suppress.

# HEARTBEAT

*What is that drumming in my new ear? Something is definitely different in here. It's thumping. Pounding. Racing. Bumping me around. A steady rhythm that clings to my soul. Can you feel it or hear it, or is it just me? A reverberating echo of who I'm meant to be. This new beat will guide me to the people I'll love and the pathways I'll choose. It's a gift from above.*

## BABY NOTES

What was your reaction to seeing and hearing your baby's heartbeat for the first time?

.................................................................................................

.................................................................................................

.................................................................................................

.................................................................................................

.................................................................................................

.................................................................................................

.................................................................................................

.................................................................................................

.................................................................................................

.................................................................................................

# week
# SEVEN

Your baby's hands and feet are
beginning to grow

# week SEVEN

*A mother's arms are more comforting than anyone else's.*
—DIANA, PRINCESS OF WALES

**I'M THIS BIG:** I'm three-fourths of an inch long.

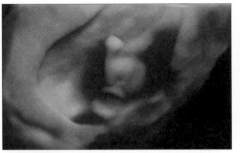 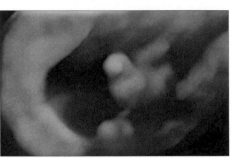

 www.tyndal.es/twwyweek7

These images are interesting because you can actually see the formation of the channel that connects baby to the yolk sac. It's called the vitelline duct. Baby is at the top of the pictures, with the cord going into his or her midsection. The baby's bottom will form to the left. The baby's head (on the right) is large and tucked down into the chest.

In the second image, the yolk sac is down low and looks like a bubble with a tiny thread connecting to baby. The heart is the largest organ right now, and if this image were moving, you could see it throbbing.

# Development

At seven weeks, I already have some reflex actions. I'm curled up with my head on my chest. My arms and legs are getting longer. My hands and feet are beginning to grow. My intestines and pancreas are forming. My cartilage is changing to bone. The inner parts of my ears are developing. Doctors have stopped calling me an embryo and started calling me a fetus (but you can call me Baby!).

# Rx for Health

Growth during this stage of pregnancy is due largely to development of the head. The brain and facial prominences are enlarging. Recent studies have looked at improved brain and eye development with consumption of omega-3 fatty acids.[1] Many prenatal vitamins include these. Continued use of omega-3s during breastfeeding may also aid the development of your baby's nervous system.

**NUTRITIONAL NUGGET**
Eat lots of whole grain foods. They provide you with complex carbohydrates, which give you slow-burning energy. Complex carbohydrates are usually full of fiber, which helps with constipation and may also prevent gestational diabetes. Whole grain breads, cereals, brown rice, and vegetables are also a great source of vitamin B. Vitamin $B_6$ may deter morning sickness. It also helps with baby's cell growth, as well as limb and organ formation. You should have six servings of vitamin B–rich foods every day.

## Mommy Moments

### Every Woman Has Her Fears

It's completely natural to have fears during pregnancy. If you're worried and anxious, you're not alone. But remember: You can do this. Your body can do this. And it's okay to talk about your fears and hopes for the future, like these moms:

*The whole idea of giving birth had always freaked me out, so I tackled my anxiety through research. By the time my eighth month ended, I was mentally ready and calm—partly due to the research and knowing what kind of delivery I wanted to have, and partly because I was sick of being pregnant and ready to get it over with!* —Tricia Cambron

*What excites me most about being a parent is seeing my children learn things I taught them. What worries me is that I might not put enough time and energy into my children, and I might regret it later.* —Tera Reelfs

*I was concerned about whether or not I would know what to do with this new baby. Would I be a better parent than mine were? Would I be terrible?* —Chris Barcus

*I was afraid that I would inadvertently do something, or not do something, that would harm my baby during pregnancy . . . or during the decades to follow.* —Lynne Carols

# PRENATAL POSTCARD

## Baby Makes Ten by Miriam Meyers

The room was dark enough for every three-dimensional object to cast a shadow. It should have been scary, but I welcomed this surreal time-out to reflect on the past year of my life. Was it just eighteen months ago that I prayed to find my "other half" and create a home? Now I was married to a wonderful man, and we had just been blessed with a healthy baby boy.

Pregnancy complications had forced me to deliver in the operating room. The equipment beeped and flashed, and I prayed, I thank You with my entire being. You have given me everything I have hoped for. Should You give me more children, I will consider each one a free, undeserved gift and will devote my life to working for You as a loving mother.

Fast-forward twenty years. My baby boy was now engaged. Just two months before the wedding, I discovered I was pregnant, a happy—somewhat unexpected—surprise. I was forty-three years old, and now the mother of five boys and four girls. Part of me was nervous. I knew the risks were greater as the mother aged. I knew that I had been on bed rest for a major part of my last four pregnancies. I also remembered the heartache of miscarrying.

As an observant Jew, I had been taught during my seminary year in Jerusalem that the Hebrew word for "mother"—em—is defined by the letters that comprise it. Translated, it means "the first one you trust." I smiled. I let a silent movie play in my mind.

I reexperienced the birth and childhood of each of our children and saw them as they were at present—each one a precious gift to the world. My first child was a need of mine. I now saw my children as gifts brought forth through the combined love of their Creator in heaven, my husband, and myself. This tenth "surprise" became an enormous source of joy! She was born on my husband's birthday and named after my two grandmothers. She is now an aunt to a niece and four nephews, and she knows she is the best surprise of my life!

# BIG

*Everything enormous starts small. I'm a drop in the universe, with a gallon of potential. The seed of a brilliant blossom on the vine of humanity. I'm trying, multiplying, stretching myself. Already more today than yesterday. Someday, not so far away, I'm gonna be big . . . with infinite possibilities. Don't you think?*

*I'm expanding right now with a purpose. I'll have ideas and change lives. Starting with yours. Especially yours.*

*Just wait. I'm gonna be big.*

*Someday.*

## BABY NOTES

What excites you most about becoming a mom? What are your hopes and fears regarding motherhood?

.......................................................................................................
.......................................................................................................
.......................................................................................................
.......................................................................................................
.......................................................................................................
.......................................................................................................
.......................................................................................................
.......................................................................................................

# week
# EIGHT

Exercise can benefit you and your
baby, but follow some guidelines

# week EIGHT

### I'M THIS BIG: I'm one inch long.

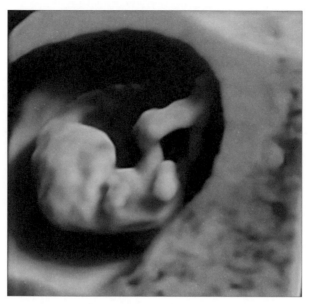

www.tyndal.es/twwyweek8

The difference between this week and last week is astonishing. In this sonogram, baby's head is on the left. The brain is rapidly developing. It functions to regulate the heartbeat, muscle movement, and breathing. Arm buds and leg buds are clearly visible. See the umbilical cord extending from the uterine wall into baby's tiny tummy?

This particular image is remarkable because if you look very closely, you can see an almost transparent film encircling baby. That is the amniotic sac! That sac will grow with baby and eventually adhere to the uterine wall.

# Development

At eight weeks, I have a face with features, and eyelids have formed. I have an upper lip and nose. Inside my mouth, teeth have started to develop. My ears are forming, inside and outside. I have elbows where my arms bend. My spine can already flex. The part of my brain that allows me to speak, see, hear, and remember is also forming.

# Rx for Health

When you exercise, baby benefits, but there are some guidelines to follow. Keeping your heart rate below 150 beats a minute is important for the baby's blood supply. When your workout is too hard, your vital organs require more blood flow, shunting it away from the baby. High-impact exercise can also stress your joints, which are more flexible during pregnancy. Low-impact exercise is best. Don't start on a new exercise routine without consulting your health-care provider.

**NUTRITIONAL NUGGET**
Proteins are the building blocks for human cells and are especially important for a developing baby. You need more protein during pregnancy. It's vital for the growth of your placenta and the development of your baby's skin and brain. According to the Institute of Medicine's guidelines, you should try to get about 1.1 gram of protein each day for every kilogram of body weight. That's at least 2.5 ounces of protein per day for an average pregnant woman.[1] Protein isn't stored in your body, so you need to eat small amounts throughout the day. Low-fat sources of protein include fish, eggs, yogurt, turkey, or chicken. If you're vegetarian, you don't have to eat meat to have a healthy pregnancy, but check with your doctor to make sure your protein intake is adequate.

## Mommy Moments

### Family Resemblance

From the moment a sperm and egg unite, an entirely unique individual is formed. Twenty-three chromosomes come from the mother, and twenty-three from the father. It's mind-boggling to think how many of your ancestors' traits may end up in the DNA combination that is your baby.

*In the 3-D sonogram of our third baby, we saw that he had my firstborn son's chubby cheeks and the same mouth. When he was born, they looked so similar. Kissable all around!* —Lucy Weber

*When we went in for my daughter's sonogram, I saw her little profile and her perfect little nose. It looked just like her daddy's.* —Maria Morris

*Our daughter looked just like me in the ultrasound. Everything about that little face, even when she cried and gave us the pouty little lip! Funny thing is, she came out looking just like Dad! She had loads of black hair and brown eyes, and I'm a blonde with blue eyes! What a little trickster she turned out to be!* —Sara Neville Fortune

*Because I had a high-risk pregnancy, we had a 3-D sonogram, and we could see that our baby girl had hair, my husband Michael's cheeks, and my chin and nose! As soon as Mckinzie was born, we could see that she did, in fact, have all those features as well as Michael's eyes.* —Heather Kahl

# PRENATAL POSTCARD

## Our Messenger from God by Brock Jones

Her name says it all. Angelia. It means "messenger from God." For nine years, our daughter's life has breathed of miracles to us. But let me back up to the beginning.

I don't think we would have our child if not for in vitro fertilization. Fina and I had been trying to get pregnant ever since we got married. We eventually learned that we couldn't conceive on our own, so we sought help.

Specialists started Fina on medicine to prepare her body for pregnancy. I endured the necessary embarrassment of having my sperm "graded." Fina's eggs were harvested and then frozen until it was time to place them in the womb.

On that emotion-filled day, we watched in wonder as an ultrasound allowed us to see our little embryo float into Fina's womb. Unbeknownst to us, Angelia's first two cells began the amazing journey of life.

The next several weeks were tense as we waited to see if one or both of the eggs would implant in the womb. After weeks of prayer and heavy emotions, we found out that one egg decided it could make the journey. We cried and thanked God for the miracle of a new life.

Eight months and two weeks later, Angelia made an early entrance into the world. It was a thank-God moment. I helped clean Angelia up and take her handprints and footprints. I still savor the incredible moment when I presented Angelia to her mom. When I look at my daughter now, I am so thankful to God for the doctors and the technology that made it possible for us to have Angelia.

# "I'M SPECIAL"

*I'm special. There's no one just like me. I'm part of you, Mom. And part of my dad. That's what makes me unique. No one right now, no one who has been, and no one who will ever be will have the same body parts, soul, and heart that were used to make me.*

## BABY NOTES

What traits do you hope your baby inherits from you? What traits from Dad?

........................................................................

........................................................................

........................................................................

........................................................................

........................................................................

........................................................................

........................................................................

........................................................................

........................................................................

........................................................................

48

# week
# NINE

Baby's muscles are
getting stronger

# week NINE

I'M THIS BIG: I'm one and one-sixteenth of an inch long, and I weigh one-sixteenth of an ounce.

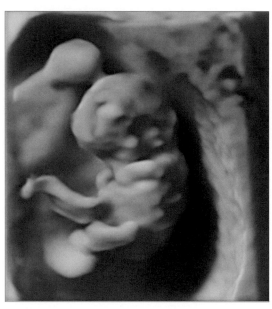

www.tyndal.es/twwyweek9

www.tyndal.es/twwyweek9

*If I had my life to live over . . . instead of wishing away nine months of pregnancy, I'd have cherished every moment and realized that the wonderment growing inside me was the only chance in life to assist God in a miracle.*
—ERMA BOMBECK, "IF I HAD MY LIFE TO LIVE OVER"

In this profile of baby's entire body, you can see the cord coming from the left side into baby's belly button. It's still big compared to the tiny babe. Just above baby's head, there is a little ball. That's the yolk sac. Soon it will dissolve, and the placenta will take over as the primary means of nourishment. Look at this little one's arms tucked into her chest. Her legs are longer now, and she is starting to exercise them.

50

# Development

By week nine, my muscles are getting stronger. You can see me move on an ultrasound. My eyes are closed. My fingers and toes have started to appear with grooves between them. The muscles in my neck are forming. You can see where my ears will be. My reflexes are developing. If you were to touch my mouth, I might pull away.

# Rx for Health

Can you believe that a limited amount of stress may be good for your baby's lung development? When Mom is stressed, she releases more of a stress-related hormone called cortisol. In small amounts, scientists think it may help baby's lungs develop. Avoid unnecessary and prolonged stress. It may cause restricted growth and preterm labor. If you feel stressed much of the time, talk to your health-care practitioner about treatment options.

**NUTRITIONAL NUGGET**
Fat is essential for a developing baby. Just don't overdo it, or the pounds will end up staying on you. Fatty foods may also contribute to morning sickness. Saturated fats may increase blood pressure. No more than 30 percent of your calories should come from fat, but don't eliminate healthy fats from your diet.

## MOMMY MOMENTS

### Mother Knows Best

From the moment you announce your pregnancy to years after you've given birth, you'll be buried in well-meaning advice. Everyone has an opinion. From baby names to nursery colors to home remedies for every ailment. Just be careful whom you listen to. Here's some positive advice from mothers:

*Sleep while you can, and enjoy every minute of your alone time! Also, write down lots of things about your pregnancy to compare with your next one.* —TERA REELFS

*Just relax. Don't listen to women who like to tell scary labor stories. Politely ask to wait until you are through labor.* —SHAWNDA TOLAND

*Get as much ready by the sixth or seventh month of pregnancy as you can. Arrange for your husband to take some vacation time when the baby is born, and accept any help that is offered.* —KIM RHODES

*Try to enjoy your pregnancy. It goes by so fast. From now on, you'll see your body in a whole new light. You might feel overweight or out of shape at times, but you'll always be grateful that this body brought a wonderful baby into the world.* —KATHY HAIVALA

# Prenatal Postcard

## Gotcha! by Kristin Morris

If there's one thing my husband and I are, it's creative. When we found out I was pregnant with our second child, we wanted to surprise our families in an unforgettable way.

We took my husband's family to an oriental restaurant and asked the waiter ahead of time to swap out their fortune cookies for ours. We planted messages in the cookies that read, "Your family will be growing in nine months." It was so funny to watch their faces as each family member cracked open the cookie.

My husband's younger sister read it first and kind of paused and looked puzzled. One by one, each family member unwrapped identical messages until everyone finally caught on.

When it was time to tell my family, we invited my mom, stepdad, grandma, and brother over for dinner. Afterward, we told them we needed a family picture for my preschooler's class. I sat everyone on the couch and said, "Okay, here we go. On the count of three. One . . . two . . . I'm pregnant!" We captured the dropped jaws, gasps, and jubilant reactions in a hilarious family photo that will forever shout, "Gotcha!"

# DON'T WORRY

*Today you're worried about the growth of my brain,*
*your swollen feet, and bad labor pain.*
*Don't.*
*I know it's the anthem of myriad mothers. You stress about*
*your babies before we even have brothers.*
*Stop.*
*Just say no to the thoughts that assail you at night. Musings over kick counts and pants that*
*are tight. You wonder if you've consumed enough omega-3s, eaten your broccoli, what*
*color green the nursery should be. Will I come out with ten toes on two perfect feet?*
*Let it go.*
*Will you lose all your baby weight? Will I gain enough?*
*Will we have any money? Will nursing be rough?*
*Breathe in. Stop obsessing. Breathe out. Release.*
*Let's think about peace and both get some sleep!*

## BABY NOTES

Write down some good advice you've received so far from friends
or family members.

........................................................................

........................................................................

........................................................................

........................................................................

........................................................................

54

# week TEN

Morning sickness affects about 50 percent of pregnant women, but generally doesn't harm baby

# week TEN

*You weren't there, and now you're here. I dreamed of you but I never knew how sweet and lovely.*
—TIFFANY LEE, "MY SWEET, MY LOVELY"

I'M THIS BIG: I'm one and a half inches long, and I weigh one-eighth of an ounce.

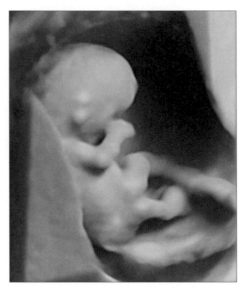

www.tyndal.es/twwyweek10

Baby is moving easily around the uterus at this point, spinning and flipping, oblivious to the pull of gravity. When your baby isn't working out, he or she is often sound asleep. This little one looks as if she is rubbing her eyes just before drifting off to dreamland. Baby is sitting on the dissolving yolk sac. She reclines against the uterine wall just as if she's sitting in a chair. The cord circles in front of her tiny feet. Look at the detail in this sweet baby's elbow and knee. The dark area surrounding the baby is amniotic fluid.

# Development

At ten weeks, you can see my umbilical cord and placenta, which are starting to transfer nutrients from you to me. The yolk sac I used for nourishment from the beginning gradually disappears. The tip of my nose is apparent on my face. Bone formation begins with the jawbone and collarbone. My hands and feet have fingers and toes now, and I'm straightening out. My head is still large compared to the rest of me. My forehead takes up a big part of my face, and my brain makes up half my weight. My genital area is forming, but a sonogram cannot yet determine my sex.

# Rx for Health

Morning sickness starts as early as six weeks but tends to peak around nine weeks. It affects about 50 percent of pregnant women but in general doesn't affect baby. It's thought to be caused by increases in the levels of certain hormones in Mom's body. Vitamin $B_6$, frequent small meals, and some over-the-counter medications can be effective in treating symptoms. Some women find ginger tea helpful in relieving nausea. Your health-care practitioner may also recommend some oral prescription medications. Thankfully, nausea in most pregnant women diminishes after about fifteen weeks.

**NUTRITIONAL NUGGET**
There are no surefire cures for morning sickness, but here are a few suggestions that may help:

- Take your prenatal vitamin right before bedtime instead of in the morning.
- Eat some crackers and then wait a few minutes before you get out of bed.
- Eat small combinations of carbohydrates and proteins throughout the day.
- Take a walk in the fresh air. It boosts endorphins and may make you feel better.
- Avoid fats, citrus fruits, and juices, and anything with a strong smell.
- Amazingly, the taste and smell of sour foods, such as lemons or green apples, may help.
- The slow release of vitamin $B_6$ may also ease nausea. Your doctor can prescribe this vitamin.

# Mommy Moments

## That Funny Feeling Inside

You never know quite when it will hit, but when it does, if it does, watch out. A bit of nausea early in pregnancy can be slightly re-assuring. It makes you feel pregnant before you look it. But there's this fine line between embracing slight morning queasiness and fleeing to the bathroom during a romantic meal out. These moms seemed to take it in stride:

> During my first pregnancy, someone told me that gingersnaps would help ease my nausea, so on my morning commute, I was munching on them right out of the box. I then proceeded to throw them up . . . right back in the box. My next two pregnancies, I just laughed when someone mentioned gingersnaps as a cure. —MARIE RILEY

> I had a touch of nausea with my second pregnancy. Cheetos helped me! —JACQUE WILSON

> I had a few days in the beginning of my twin pregnancy where I was so sick to my stomach that it was hard to get up. One of my books recommended eating something salty and sour together before getting out of bed. So I tried pretzels and lemonade in the mornings when I felt a bit ill, and it worked. —KARA BROEKER

> When I was pregnant with my daughter, I ate strawberry Pop-Tarts every morning for weeks! Somehow they helped with the nausea. —RENEÉ VELA

58

# PRENATAL POSTCARD

## In Sickness and in Public Bathrooms
## by Jennifer Anderson

For me, the glow of pregnancy was more like a clammy sheen that I sponged off my upper lip every morning after I hung my head over the toilet bowl. Morning sickness hit early and often and lasted for about eight months. I tried everything. Licorice, crackers, dry cereal, Popsicles . . . to no avail. I threw up in parking lots and grassy spots all over the city. But the worst place I ever lost it was the unisex bathroom at the gas station down the street.

My husband was filling up the car when a wave of nausea hit me. I started pacing, willing myself to avoid a visit to the dirty, one-room hovel that seemed to mock me from the side of the building. But I didn't have much choice. It was either the hovel or the trash can beside the gas pump.

For five minutes, I retched. The echo off the concrete walls sounded like an exorcist taming a wild beast. When it was over, I lifted my head to the mirror and saw broken blood vessels under both eyes and mascara running down my cheeks. I calmly wiped up the mess, leaving the place cleaner than when I entered.

I opened the bathroom door, stepped into the sunlight, and inhaled. A line of anxious bathroom waiters gawked. I didn't even look pregnant yet. I quickly lowered my eyes and thought, If I was in that line, and I saw and heard what those people just did, I would turn around and run!

## "MY NOSE"

*Look carefully. Do you see anything different about me? Here, I'll turn this way.
There! Can't you see it? It's right in the middle of my face . . . It's my nose! Hoo-wee!
I have one now. It's just a bump, but I wonder what it will look like someday. Big
as a lump? Long as a tree? Or will I get one like yours, Mommy? Maybe I'll have
my great-grandpa's nose—the one with the hook on the end. Who knows?*

## BABY NOTES

Have you experienced morning sickness during your pregnancy?
What helped?

..................................................................................
..................................................................................
..................................................................................
..................................................................................
..................................................................................
..................................................................................
..................................................................................
..................................................................................
..................................................................................

# week ELEVEN

Your baby's heart beats about
160 times per minute

# week ELEVEN

*Baby, baby, I'm taken with the notion to love you with the sweetest of devotion.*
—AMY GRANT, "BABY BABY"

I'M THIS BIG: I'm two and three-sixteenths of an inch long, and I weigh five-sixteenths of an ounce.

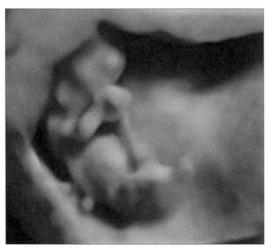

www.tyndal.es/twwyweek11

Peekaboo! In this photo, baby seems to be covering her little eyes in a game she is sure to enjoy in about nine months. This baby is nestled into the side of the uterus. There is plenty of room for movement and growth, and it's a good thing because baby is growing more than a half inch per week. If *you* grew this fast, you would be two to three inches taller by the end of this month! Baby's ears are low set on the head at this point. As the head grows, the ears will center up.

# DEVELOPMENT

At eleven weeks, I kick and jab. This helps my muscles and bones get stronger. I can touch my hand to my face. Sometimes I get hiccups. I can yawn, stretch, and swallow. My fingernails are starting to appear. My placenta has fully formed and helps regulate the temperature in your uterus. My brain has developed to the point where I am probably already right- or left-hand dominant. My heart now beats about 160 times a minute. Later, as my nervous system matures, my heart will come under the control of my brain. It will slow down and beat more steadily.

# Rx for Health

Between ten and thirteen weeks, your health-care practitioner may offer to give you a blood test and ultrasound to determine whether your baby is at risk for genetic disorders, such as Down syndrome. All women are offered this test, but it's often recommended for women over thirty-five, as well as women who may be at risk due to complications in previous pregnancies. Testing is optional and is usually covered by insurance. If the test shows a possible problem with the baby, more invasive tests are offered to provide more information. Further testing is more accurate, but it also poses a potential risk to the baby.

**NUTRITIONAL NUGGET**
If you want your baby to receive adequate oxygen through your blood, get enough iron. Iron is necessary for your body to make healthy red blood cells, which carry oxygen through the placenta to the baby. The recommended daily amount of iron is around 27 mg.[1] Iron deficiency is the most common cause of maternal anemia or a low red blood-cell count. Anemia makes the mother extremely tired. For the baby, it increases the risk of low birthweight, preterm birth, and mortality. It's best to get iron naturally through lean red meat, dried apricots, prunes, and leafy, green vegetables. Many breakfast cereals are also fortified with iron.

## MOMMY MOMENTS

### Movin' 'n' Groovin'

We've all heard the urban legends about marathon mamas who can outrun a band of ninja warriors even with nine months of baby flesh bouncing around inside them. Seriously, that kind of workout isn't for most of us, but breaking a regular sweat has its benefits. Here's how some supermoms stuck to their fitness routines:

*I've done martial arts most of my life and continued to teach karate throughout my pregnancy. We have to wear a uniform called a gi, which seemed to stretch beyond any reasonable proportion when I was in my ninth month! Although I felt I looked ridiculous, the stretching and flexibility and strength training I had built up helped during labor and delivery.*
—KRISTA "FUNKY MAMA" EYLER

*I did the elliptical machine at the gym three times a week up until my delivery. I also played tennis until I was eight months pregnant. That was funny looking. The only thing I couldn't do while pregnant was walk. I would get Braxton Hicks contractions just walking down the street!* —SARAH GRAY

*I taught Zumba all through my pregnancy. When Madeline was born (a week late), we discovered she loves movement. As a newborn, she was crying one night around six o'clock. I told my husband to bounce her, because it was the time she would normally have been in Zumba class. She quieted down immediately!* —TRICIA DAVENPORT

# PRENATAL POSTCARD

## Strong Start, Easy Finish
## by Laura Bowling

I've always enjoyed exercise, but when I became pregnant for the first time, I decided to try something new—deep-water aerobics. I was fourteen weeks along when I strapped on the flotation belt for the first time and entered ten feet of water. The workout was great cardio and muscle toning with no impact on my joints. I continued the routine into my fortieth week, moving the belt up as my baby grew. Instead of feeling tired and heavy in my third trimester, I felt great. I was actually growing stronger.

I wasn't the only one who enjoyed the workout. My baby seemed to like it too. She was still, maybe even asleep, through the routine, but when it was over, she became active. I worked out in the evenings, so by the time I went to bed at night, my daughter had settled down. We both slept well.

I appreciated the effects of my regular workouts most of all on delivery day. As contractions came, I endured. When the nurse told me to push, I could feel my abdominals helping my baby make her way into the world. When Katelyn emerged, she was strong and alert.

Exercise doesn't make every pregnancy and delivery easy. It doesn't make every baby perfect. But it helped keep my weight down and my energy up, and I would do it again in a heartbeat.

# BODY BUILDER

*Hi, Mom! Look at this. I'm the size of a bean. But I have elbows and rib bones. My biceps are lean. I'm not chillin' in here with nothing to do . . . wasting the day . . . waiting on you. I arch and spin. I bounce and high-step. I'm a busy bodybuilder just loggin' some reps. My form here is weightless. My abs are quite buff. While you are pooching out, I'm pumpin' up.*

## BABY NOTES

Have you incorporated any exercise into your routine? What does a "day in the life of you" look like during your pregnancy?

........................................................................

........................................................................

........................................................................

........................................................................

........................................................................

........................................................................

........................................................................

........................................................................

........................................................................

........................................................................

66

# week
# TWELVE

Drink more water! Your blood
flow increases while pregnant

# week TWELVE

*What delights us in visible beauty is the invisible.*
—Marie von Ebner-Eschenbach, Austrian Author

### I'm This Big: I'm three inches long, and I weigh five-eighths of an ounce.

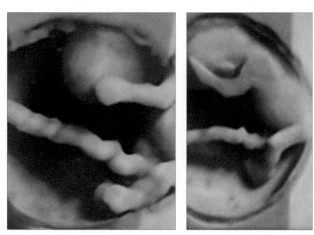

www.tyndal.es/twwyweek12

In only nine weeks, your baby has grown from two tiny cells . . . to this! You can clearly see the definition between the amniotic sac and the uterine wall. Baby will start to push that uterus out! Notice the detailed coil in the cord. It is growing longer. The cord contains one vein that carries nutrient-rich blood and oxygen to the baby, and two arteries that carry depleted oxygen back to the placenta. Typically, the umbilical cord will be approximately the same length as your baby measures from the top of her head to her bottom. The cord grows with the baby. At birth, the average umbilical cord is twenty inches long and one to two centimeters wide.

# Development

By week twelve, my brain is sending messages to the rest of my body. I might be able to suck my thumb, and my vocal cords are beginning to develop. The doctor can listen to my heartbeat by placing Doppler equipment outside your abdomen. My face has a very human profile now that my chin has more fully developed. Some hair is growing on my body.

# Rx for Health

For most women, morning sickness may have subsided by now and they are starting to feel better, and many are asking questions about sex. It's safe during all trimesters of pregnancy, unless you're having complications. In some instances, such as vaginal bleeding or preterm labor, you should abstain from sex. As your body changes, you may need to experiment with different positions during sex for comfort. Check with your health-care provider if you have any concerns.

**NUTRITIONAL NUGGET**
Everyone is always telling us to drink more water. During pregnancy, this is especially important. Your blood flow increases by as much as 50 percent, and so does the fluid in your tissue. To support that, your system needs water. Try for about ten eight-ounce cups per day.[1] This includes water and other beverages you may be drinking, such as milk and juice. Drinking water keeps your blood pressure down and prevents swelling and urinary tract infections. Water also gives your baby more room for growth in the uterus and reduces the risk of preterm labor. It's also needed for regular bowel movements and helps your body process fiber.

# MOMMY MOMENTS

## Womb Window

Many times women are allowed one ultrasound around mid-pregnancy. But every once in a while, your health-care provider may order an earlier peek at your baby. What you see might surprise you.

*We had an early sonogram with Noah at twelve weeks. He was almost two inches long, so lifelike in the sonogram picture. I never imagined I would see a blob, but I wasn't prepared to see a baby with toes and fingers so early! It was amazing!* —CHRISTIANE BRANSTROM

*Our first look at the baby was about fifteen weeks along. From the moment the screen came alive, I was mesmerized. That sweet baby was kicking and waving at us. That stole my heart then and there. I took the black-and-white printout and showed it to everyone I knew. Then I framed it and put it on my desk.* —LYNNE CAROLS

*The first time we had an ultrasound, it was strange seeing the shape of the baby—it looked so alien with a giant head and tiny body. I remember watching movement and being told, "That's the heart beating" and "Those are the kidneys, brain, spine . . ." It was amazing being able to see inside this little person when we didn't even know what her outside was going to look like.* —TRICIA CAMBRON

# PRENATAL POSTCARD

## Ultrasound Shock! by Rebecca Ishum

Lying on the table in the dark room, I was anxious for the sonographer to find a heartbeat. After dealing with infertility, being pregnant was a miracle. The midwife cautioned me that it might be too early to see anything; however, I was so afraid that I would lose the baby, she agreed to look. The grainy image projected on the screen didn't help calm my fears. I had no idea what we were looking at and had to wait for any hint of well-being from the woman running the wand over my stomach.

My heart dropped when she needed to switch to a vaginal ultrasound. I glanced at my husband across the room. Why couldn't she find our baby? The sonographer cut through my thoughts with the news that there were indeed heartbeats. Heartbeats? Not just one heartbeat but three, and an extra sac that could possibly contain a fourth.

Lying on the table, I started shaking from the fear that immediately engulfed me. Ten days later, with hardly enough time to wrap my mind around three babies, the sonographer found a fourth baby, alive and well.

We were having quadruplets. At that point, I realized that I felt incredibly angry and betrayed by God. First, no children; now four. How is that fair? I was supposed to be overjoyed at being pregnant and eagerly anticipate my due date. Instead, I just felt angry, used, and abandoned by the One who was always supposed to have my back.

However, God was gracious and patient with me and allowed me to question and cry out my fears to Him. And that's when the fierce love of a mother started to fill my heart. I still had questions and fears. I still knew that we were facing an impossible task, but I knew that I would do anything for my children to give them the best chance of survival. And I knew that God was going to walk our impossible path with us.

When my kids were finally born at twenty-seven weeks, six days, I was so grateful that God chose me and my husband to parent them. A blessing I didn't understand at first ended up being more than I ever could have hoped for.

(You can visit Rebecca's website at www.abeautifulruckus.com.)

## "GUESS WHAT I HAVE?"

*Do do do. I have a surprise for you. Dee dee dee. It's something about only me. Can you guess what it is? I'll give you some hints. It can get me in trouble or set me free. It's a very small part of my identity. They circle around like a cranny and nook. On the day I'm born, they'll go in my book. Dum dum dum. It's right on the end of my thumb. It's my fingerprints.*

## BABY NOTES

Were there any surprises discovered at your ultrasound? Was your baby active or just taking it easy? What would you like to remember from the experience?

........................................................................................................

........................................................................................................

........................................................................................................

........................................................................................................

........................................................................................................

........................................................................................................

........................................................................................................

........................................................................................................

........................................................................................................

# week
# THIRTEEN

You may be having cravings!
Ice cream, anyone?

# week THIRTEEN

**I'M THIS BIG:** I'm three and a half inches long, and I weigh one ounce.

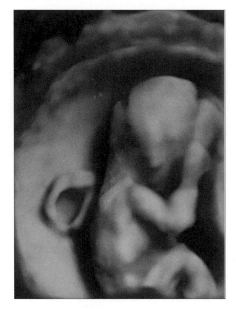

www.tyndal.es/twwyweek13

In this image, the yolk sac is dissolving behind baby's back. Baby is now completely dependent on the placenta and umbilical cord for nutrients. You can also see the angle of this baby's rib cage around the spine. Baby's still pretty skinny, but his weight has increased significantly this week, and baby will start putting on some fat in the second trimester. Your baby is kicking a lot at this point in the pregnancy, but you probably can't feel it quite yet.

*The hand that rocks the cradle is the hand that rules the world.*
—WILLIAM ROSS WALLACE

# Development

All of my organs are working by now, and most of my parts are fully formed. I just need to grow. My body is growing faster than my head. My facial features are becoming more distinctive. My fingers and toes have a place for my nails to start growing.

# Rx for Health

Starting in the second trimester, you may begin to have some cravings. Most are harmless, but some can indicate a medical problem. For example, if a woman is severely iron deficient, she may have unnatural cravings, such as a craving for dirt, clay, cornstarch, laundry detergent, or baking soda. More commonly, iron-deficient women crave ice. If you experience any of these cravings, contact your physician. Usually an iron supplement will alleviate these unhealthy cravings.

**NUTRITIONAL NUGGET**
There is no scientific evidence that pregnant women crave certain foods based on the nutritional needs of the baby. Cravings are most likely due to hormonal changes. Most mothers have cravings for certain foods and aversions to others, especially in the first trimester. If your cravings are for healthy foods, give in. If you just want ice cream all the time, try to find a more nutritious substitute, such as milk or fruit.

Most food cravings and aversions weaken by the fourth month of pregnancy. If they persist, it may be a sign of a deeper emotional need that demands attention.

## MOMMY MOMENTS

### Glorious Food!

It's not just pickles and ice cream that call to us in the middle of the night. Our inner yearnings are as unique as the babies we're carrying. They can draw us and push us away all in one motion. Can you relate to any of the following cravings?

*I craved milk. It just sounded and tasted so good!* —LAURISA MYERS

*I wanted apples all the time.* —NOREEN DUPRIEST

*During both my pregnancies, at around four months, I craved steak.* —SHAWNDA TOLAND

*I had to have beef and cheese enchiladas every day!* —HEATHER ENGLAND

*I craved bagel sandwiches with cucumbers at lunchtime.* —KIM RHODES

*One night I ate a whole jar of green olives!* —CHRISTINA BURKE

*I craved anything with vinegar—salad dressing, chips, mustard.* —MARIANNE HERING

*During my second pregnancy, I craved French dip sandwiches and Vietnamese food!* —JULIA ASHWORTH

*I craved crunchy tacos during my first pregnancy!* —JENNY OJALA

# PRENATAL POSTCARD

## A Little Fruity by Brandy Bruce

I've always been fascinated by the cravings pregnant women have, and I wondered whether I'd have any once I became pregnant. The answer was definitely yes! I've never been one to drink fruity drinks, but not long after I found out I was pregnant, I started having an intense thirst for orange soda! I wanted orange soda morning, noon, and night. My husband had to make regular trips to the grocery store for the stuff. Absolutely nothing tasted better.

After my daughter, Ashtyn, was born, I poured a glass and quickly realized that my passion for orange fruitiness was gone. The craving had vanished. Three years later, when I found out I was pregnant with my second child, my husband and I wondered whether the orange-soda passion would return. But something else sounded even better: strawberry soda!

The only thing I wanted to drink was strawberry soda. One evening after a particularly exhausting day, I burst into tears. My husband, Jeff, came running, saying, "What happened? What can I do?"

I sniffled. "We're out of strawberry soda."

He was out the door in a flash and heading down the street to the local grocery store.

But as soon as my son, Lincoln, was born, just as before, my craving ceased. Strawberry soda? No thanks.

My husband and I laugh at the fact that I seem to have fruity pregnancies. If we have a third baby, I fully expect to start longing for grape soda!

# "ARE YOU HUNGRY?"

*I know. It's the middle of the night. Way past dinnertime. But I've worked up quite an appetite. I'm already awake. Aren't you? I need some nutrition. How about that leftover stew? Or pasta or carrots. Doesn't that sound yummy? Maybe you could send some peanut butter and jelly down to your tummy. I'm not a bit picky at this point in the game. Just get me some ice cream or grapes . . . down the drain. Whatever you do, don't go back to sleep. I'm small, but I'm hungry. I need something to eat.*

## BABY NOTES

What are your cravings or your favorite things to eat? What can't you stomach?

..................................................................................
..................................................................................
..................................................................................
..................................................................................
..................................................................................
..................................................................................
..................................................................................
..................................................................................
..................................................................................

# week FOURTEEN

Your baby's fingers can
curl into fists

# week FOURTEEN

**I'M THIS BIG:** I'm five inches long, and I weigh two ounces.

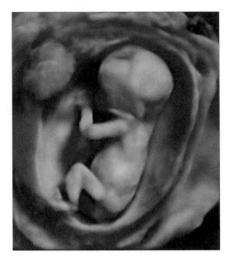

www.tyndal.es/twwyweek14

What a perfect view of baby cradled inside the layers of the uterus. Mom's uterine wall provides a hammock of support that feels soft and secure. The inside layer is the amniotic sac; the second layer is the muscle of the uterus. The placenta looks like a cloud on the upper left. The umbilical cord is over the baby's left shoulder. This little one is forming a small amount of fat around his or her midsection.

The fontanels in the baby's head are forming. Those are the membrane-filled areas between the bones in the cranium that allow for the brain to grow. At birth, the "soft spots" allow the head to slightly compress so baby can pass safely through the birth canal. If a diagnostic sonogram is done at this point, a doctor can check baby's stomach, bladder, and kidneys to make sure everything is in working order.

# Development

By week fourteen, my fingers can curl into fists. I smile and frown. My sex is now clearly distinguishable externally, but it's still very difficult to see on a sonogram. If I'm a boy, I'm producing testosterone. If I'm a girl, I'm already producing my own eggs. My neck is well defined and getting longer so my chin doesn't have to rest on my chest. I have plenty of space to move around in the amniotic fluid. When you poke at your stomach, I can move away.

# Rx for Health

Health-care providers can usually tell if your uterus is measuring slightly larger than normal. If that's the case, an ultrasound is ordered. The discrepancy could be due to multiple babies. If you're having more than one baby, you'll have numerous tests to monitor your pregnancy. A month from now, you'll have a high-level screening ultrasound. There is a higher risk of preterm labor with multiples, so your provider might measure your cervix by ultrasound. With multiple babies, you're likely to go into labor earlier than the usual thirty-seven to forty-two weeks. Even if you haven't started labor, your provider may advise delivery of your babies before term if complications, such as low amniotic fluid or problems with the babies' growth, start to develop.

**NUTRITIONAL NUGGET**
Caffeine is a diuretic that is passed through the placenta to your baby. If you have too much of it, it can wash other vital nutrients, like iron and calcium, away from your baby and out of your body. Don't ever replace water with a caffeinated beverage. Caffeine is also a stimulant. It causes your heart rate to increase and dilates your blood vessels.

If you must have caffeine, limit your intake to no more than 200 mg per day.[1] That's roughly the amount in twelve ounces of automatic drip coffee. Gourmet coffee and java often have more than double the amount of caffeine as drip coffee. Other sources of caffeine are soda, tea, chocolate, energy drinks, and some over-the-counter medicines.

# Mommy Moments

## Prenatal Prayer

Even moms who have never thought much about God can get a little spiritual during pregnancy. Prenatal parenting comes with some anxiety. Prayer is an antidote. To some mothers, it's just a deep thought; to others it's a full-on conversation. When we can do no more, there's hope that Someone else still can.

*I prayed over Sylas almost every day while I was pregnant. I asked God to cause my son to grow healthy and keep him from harm. I asked that my children would come to know God at an early age. I prayed for their future spouses and much more. I also asked that we would have wisdom to raise them.* —Jacque Wilson

*My dad prayed over both of my babies when they were born. He blessed them as Isaac blessed Jacob and Esau in the book of Genesis. He then prayed that they would tell others about God. Next he prayed for their health and that they would be a blessing to their parents.* —Amanda Chapman

*The blessing I say every Friday while lighting my Sabbath candles includes unborn children. During labor, God is close, so it's especially worthwhile to pray. When I was in labor, I even thought about the women in the hospital with me. I asked God to help them all.* —Miriam Meyers

*For each pregnancy, it was encouraging to pray with my husband that the baby would be safe and delivery would go smoothly. Prayer helped me so much.* —Samantha Krieger

# PRENATAL POSTCARD

## Praying for Closure by R. J. Thesman

My husband and I tried for six years to get pregnant. Month after month . . . nothing. Then finally, unbelievably, the test was positive. But I lost my baby boy through miscarriage. Two years later, his sister followed the same journey. In my womb for twelve weeks . . . then gone. But I couldn't give up. I wanted to be a mother.

So when I announced another pregnancy after two more years, the ladies of my prayer group started a prayer chain that included practically every woman in our small town. The specific prayer was, "God, close up Rebecca's womb so that her baby cannot slip out, and please make this a successful pregnancy."

At that point, I felt numb and could only pray, "Please, God." So I was grateful for those other women who seemed to have more strength and more faith than I. Although the doctor couldn't find a definitive reason why I had lost my first babies, I stayed in bed for six months and struggled with morning sickness the entire time. Sick but grateful for each day that my baby still grew inside me.

Our son was two weeks late. Finally the contractions started, and when they were five minutes apart, we headed for the hospital.

After sixteen hours of labor, which included three and a half hours of pushing, I grabbed my husband's shirt and said, "Tell them to stop praying! The baby can come out now!"

The doctor finally had to use forceps to bring our son into the world. Those ladies really knew how to pray.

# A SMILE

*What's this feeling on my face? My lips spreading out? It's not a pout. It feels pretty good, this new move of mine. It may be a reflex that I need to refine. I hope you smile, too, when you think of me. I'm still pretty small . . . but sweet as a pea.*

## BABY NOTES

Take a few moments to write out a prayer for your baby.

..................................................................................

..................................................................................

..................................................................................

..................................................................................

..................................................................................

..................................................................................

..................................................................................

..................................................................................

..................................................................................

..................................................................................

..................................................................................

# week FIFTEEN

Your baby can suck his or her
thumb by this point

# week FIFTEEN

## I'M THIS BIG: I'm five and a half inches long, and I weigh three ounces.

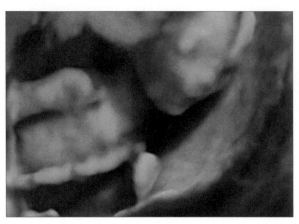

www.tyndal.es/twwyweek15

This little one is lying on her side with her cheek against the pillow of her mom's uterine wall. The umbilical cord is across her chest and draped over one shoulder. Bones are getting harder, but baby's skin is still pretty thin, almost translucent. Very fine hair, called lanugo, is starting to form. Throughout your pregnancy, it will cover your baby's little body. Most of it falls off before baby is born.

*I am a sacred vessel, alright? All you've got in your stomach is Taco Bell.*
—JUNO MACGUFF, IN THE MOVIE *Juno*

# Development

At fifteen weeks, my skin is thin. I can suck my thumb. You can see me free-floating in an ultrasound. I have a full skeleton, and my bones are getting stronger.

The hair follicles on my head are already forming their own precise pattern. According to a report in *Advanced Neonatal Care*, the number of follicles depends on my race. If I'm African American, I have up to 150,000. Asian babies have up to 120,000, and Caucasian babies have between 100,000 and 150,000. Inside the womb, I will shed and regrow my hair twice before birth. Eight to twelve weeks after I'm born, I may lose all my hair again. But rest assured, it will grow back and probably fill in completely by the time I'm two years old.

# Rx for Health

Most moms will begin to feel small flutterings in their abdomen by twenty weeks. Some women recognize it earlier if this isn't their first baby. If the placenta is on the front side of the uterus, a mom may not feel movements until much later, and maybe not as frequently until the baby is bigger.

**NUTRITIONAL NUGGET**
Although sugar-sweetened soft drinks may cause you to put on weight, think twice about substituting diet soda for them during pregnancy. A six-year study involving 59,334 pregnant women indicated that daily consumption of artificially sweetened soft drinks may cause preterm birth.[1] To be safe, avoid regular use of artificial sweeteners.

# Mommy Moments

## Belly Laughs

Admit it. Pregnancy is funny. For the noble cause of reproducing life, we are willing to swell and barf and stretch and waddle. It's humiliating but often hilarious. Have a few belly laughs with these mamas as they celebrate the uncomfortable joys of pregnancy by lettin' it all hang out:

*One of my more memorable funnies was encountering another pregnant woman in a Kmart store. We were both in the last weeks, and it was comical trying to get by each other without knocking numerous items off the shelves. We ended up rubbing bellies in passing.* —Diana Berger

*The uncontrollable flatulence in pregnancy! I was running out of ways to pretend it wasn't me. Like "Oh, my chair is so squeaky today!" or "My shoes keep making that crazy noise!"* —Tess Koppelman

*I'm fifteen weeks pregnant with twins. My two-year-old is always lifting up my shirt, fascinated by my "big belly button"! So much for my self-esteem!* —Heidi Maggio

*At seven months pregnant, I was huge and totally stuck in the ladies' room at a Colorado Rockies game. The stalls were so narrow that when my protruding belly and I got in, I had to step up onto the toilet seat to get the door closed! When I finished, I spent about five minutes maneuvering around in the tiny stall. I finally had to hang on to the wall over the toilet and pull the door open with my foot!* —Sharron Stewart

# Prenatal Postcard

## Roses in Bloom by Lucy Weber

It was my first pregnancy, so birthing classes sounded like a good idea. Natural birthing classes sounded even better. The first night, my husband and I sat on the wooden floor with the smell of incense wafting around our heads, convinced that this was the peaceful way babies were meant to be welcomed into the world. Our makeup-free instructor with the curly, brown tresses and flowing clothes put on a movie to set the stage. Wildlife giving birth in the woods. We yuppies now knew natural was the only pure course of action.

Sometimes the classes made my husband and me a little giggly. We were a bit uncomfortable with some of the things we were asked to do. One night we were going through some relaxation techniques. The instructor said, "shift your focus from pain to something positive." The birthing partners were asked to imagine along with us.

It was often too much for my very traditional husband. He leaned over and whispered, "It doesn't matter how hard I try, I cannot imagine my cervix opening like a rose." The tenderly constructed, organic mood crumbled. We stifled laughter, desperate not to wilt anyone else's imaginary blooms.

Weeks later, in a tiny, sterile hospital room that smelled more of bleach than lavender oil, hours of labor that eventually stopped progressing made me succumb to the enemy. The epidural. And am I glad I did!

But my husband and I will never forget the vision of his blooming cervix. In fact, he has picked the perfect moment to revisit the joke in each of my subsequent pregnancies.

# THE WAVE

*I waved today. Did you see me? I spread out my fingers and stretched my arm high and moved it up and then down. It was a secret signal to all of you out there that I'm safe and sound. You didn't know I had grown so big and was capable of such cool tricks . . . until I kicked. And that showed you and them that I'm no wee little bit!*

## BABY NOTES

So far, what have been the best and the hardest parts of your pregnancy? Have you had any funny, memorable moments you want to remember? If so, write those down here.

..............................................................................................

..............................................................................................

..............................................................................................

..............................................................................................

..............................................................................................

..............................................................................................

..............................................................................................

..............................................................................................

..............................................................................................

# week
## SIXTEEN

Your baby's head makes up half
of his or her body length

# week SIXTEEN

**I'M THIS BIG:** I'm six inches long, and I weigh about four ounces.

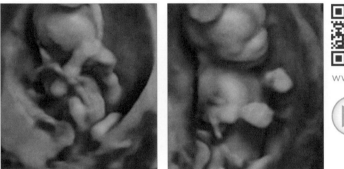

www.tyndal.es/twwyweek16

Doesn't this baby look as if she's playing peekaboo? Notice the clear view of the fontanels in the cranium, made more prominent because of so little fat. In the second image, you can also see the umbilical cord going right into baby's belly button. Most babies look very similar at this point in development. Their small features have yet to take on specific character traits. Baby's eyes are still closed at this point, but the mouth opens and closes as baby takes in and expels amniotic fluid.

*If nature had arranged that husbands and wives should have children alternatively, there would never be more than three in a family.*
—LAURENCE HOUSMAN, ENGLISH PLAYWRIGHT

# Development

At sixteen weeks, my head makes up almost half of my body length. I can hold it erect. My eyes are now in front of my head instead of more on the side. My ears are also close to their final positions. My legs are well developed. My fingernails are growing, and my toenails are starting to form. I have eyelashes and brows. I might even have some hair on my head.

# Rx for Health

There's an old wives' tale that says if a pregnant mom has severe heartburn, her baby likely will be born with a head full of hair. Recent studies indicate that might not be a myth. According to a study from Johns Hopkins University, heartburn in moms-to-be may have something to do with high levels of the hormone estrogen that cause the sphincter at the bottom of the esophagus to relax. This can not only cause a mom's heartburn, but it can also increase her baby's hair.[1] Other studies also show that estrogen may influence fetal hair growth.

Small, frequent meals, as well as avoiding greasy and spicy foods, may relieve heartburn. Over-the-counter medications and prescription medications can also help. Consult your health-care provider before taking any medication.

**NUTRITIONAL NUGGET**
Recent studies are giving pregnant women a good reason to eat chocolate. It may decrease your risk of preeclampsia. Preeclampsia is an increase in blood pressure that causes swelling in your face and hands. It can harm the baby by causing oxygen deprivation.

Research shows that chocolate decreases blood pressure by improving blood-vessel function.[2] So eat three guiltless servings a week of chocolate chips, dark chocolate bars, or hot cocoa.

## MOMMY MOMENTS
### Dreamland

Maybe it comes from worrying about motherhood. Or maybe it's because we spend so much brainpower wondering about that new life nestled centimeters below the surface of our tummies. As many of us drift off to sleep, we take our daylight obsessions into dreamland to figure them out. Somewhere in the darkness, sandwiched in the snippets between potty breaks and pregnancy pillows, our subconscious states can get a little wacky.

*I had a dream that I gave birth to a walking, talking toddler. I just skipped the whole baby thing.* —TESS KOPPELMAN

*Just days after I told my husband we were expecting a baby, he dreamed that we were having twin boys. I was sixteen weeks pregnant when our doctor heard two heartbeats thumping away in dream-affirming unison. My husband was validated. I was scared spitless. One week later, in an ultrasound, we discovered they were indeed boys.* —JOANNA MAY

*I dreamed I was having a cat. I am not fond of cats. In the dream, my ever-positive mom said, "No matter what your baby is, you will love it."* —INGRID BRUNS

*I dreamed multiple times that I gave birth to turtles!* —TRACI DAVIS

*I had several dreams where my two older children would travel Magic School Bus–style through my belly button. They would tell their little brother all about our family.* —COURTNEY BELLEMERE

# PRENATAL POSTCARD

Dreaming of Hannah by April Hawley

I had no idea I was pregnant. We had a nine-month-old who didn't sleep more than three hours at a time, and pregnancy was the furthest thing from my mind. I went to sleep one night and had the strangest dream. It was dark; I only heard the sound of a voice saying, "You're pregnant. She's going to be a girl. You're going to name her Hannah Grace. Trust in the Lord; everything is going to be okay." When I woke up, I was honestly a little freaked out by the dream. I shared the dream with my husband the next day. He asked me to get a pregnancy test, just in case.

It was positive.

I could hardly believe it. Pregnant! All I could picture was a nine-month-old baby and a newborn. I was scared, nervous, excited, shocked—a whole lot of mixed emotions. I just couldn't picture what my life would look like, but I knew I had to trust God. My husband was working from home and was in a meeting so I couldn't share the news right away. I was pacing back and forth, wearing down the carpet, waiting for him to come out. When he finally surfaced I looked into his eyes, crying, and told him that we were having another baby. He laughed with excitement and joy. When it was time for the ultrasound that would tell us our baby's gender, I was feeling skeptical, but I hadn't forgotten that dream. I held my husband's hand in anticipation and the ultrasound technician announced, "It's a girl!"

I cried in disbelief. My dream was coming true.

A few months later, I was holding my daughter. Of course we named her Hannah Grace.

# SIXTEEN WEEKS OLD

*Yeah! I'm sixteen weeks old today. Hey. The big four months. Half a foot long, and that's no bunk. Some of my stuff still needs some tweaking. But it's all there. I might even have some hair. I feel pretty good. I hope you do too, Mom. Those first months of puking were really a bomb. I know I'm in water, but that was off base. You'd heave, and I'd tumble all over the place. Sixteen weeks old! That's something to celebrate. I'll keep on growing, and you eat some cake.*

## BABY NOTES

Have you had any strange dreams during your pregnancy? What have you been dreaming about?

.................................................................
.................................................................
.................................................................
.................................................................
.................................................................
.................................................................
.................................................................
.................................................................

# week
# SEVENTEEN

Keep eating your fruits
and veggies!

# week SEVENTEEN

I'M THIS BIG: I'm seven inches long, and I weigh five ounces.

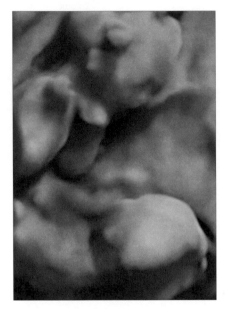

www.tyndal.es/twwyweek17

The sonographer revealed to this first-time mother that she was having twins! The boys are in separate sacs but interacted a lot during this ultrasound. They often reached for one another. In this image, one baby is high in the mom's uterus and one is low. They are facing each other. Mom witnessed an early wrestling match of reaching and punching between the boys—a match she will soon referee for a few decades. The image of the lower baby seems to peer inside his brain. This is just the way the sonar is bouncing around the uterus. Rest assured, the back of his head is fully intact.

# Development

At seventeen weeks, I'm slowly gaining weight. My movements are more voluntary, often as a result of my brain sending messages to my nervous system. I have my own fingerprints and footprints. They're uniquely me!

# Rx for Health

Most women who experience preterm labor have no identified risk factors. Sometimes early labor can be prevented. If you smoke, quitting may help you carry your baby to term. If you do experience some early signs of labor, your physician may help by giving you a progesterone supplement or performing a cerclage (a stitch around the cervix). Discuss any concerns about your risk for preterm labor with your physician.

**NUTRITIONAL NUGGET**
We all know that fruits and vegetables are good for us, but some pack more nutritional value than others. An easy way to choose the best for you and your baby is to pick brightly colored produce. For instance, spinach and romaine lettuce have far more vitamins than iceberg lettuce. Bright-orange or red foods usually contain vitamin A. Dark-green, leafy vegetables are loaded with vitamin C and iron. Raw broccoli contains folic acid. Try to eat at least five servings of brightly colored fruits and vegetables each day.

# Mommy Moments

## A Sign of Things to Come

It's weird to think that what's happening inside our wombs now will recur once baby is born. But it's true. As these moms discovered, our babies are already developing preferences and traits that may surface postbirth.

*During two of my pregnancies, we saw in the sonogram that our kids slept with one hand across their chests and one hand beside their heads. They both did the same after birth.* —Christiane Branstrom

*Our son's head was so low that we couldn't get a good look at his face, but the sonographer could tell that he was sucking on his hand. He must have really liked that, because he had a red mark on his hand when he was born!* —Cindi Chien

*Spencer kicked a lot before he was born. Now he is an excellent soccer player.* —Leslie Alford

*When I was pregnant with my son, Drew, he seemed to get very still during the praise and worship part of our church service, then he would kick like crazy when it was over! To this day, he loves music!* —Danielle Good

# Prenatal Postcard

## "I'm All Right" by Melissa Papish

It happened in an instant. During an ultrasound, my thirty-one-week-old son raised his left hand and made a perfect circle with his thumb and forefinger. Then he held his three other fingers high. He was going to be okay! His prebirth message was a great relief.

But let me rewind so you'll understand just how much that moment meant to us. Two years before, we were blessed with the arrival of our daughter, Brinley. She was one in forty thousand babies born with symbrachydactyly, a congenital hand anomaly. On her left hand, she has a partial thumb and nubbins where her other fingers should have been. It was a complete shock to us. I had several sonograms during my pregnancy, and no one had ever noticed. Brinley is perfectly healthy, just a bit different, which makes her uniquely wonderful to us.

When we discovered I was pregnant with our second child, our doctor wanted us to have a level-two ultrasound, given our history with Brinley. At twenty weeks, we found out we were having a little boy, but the maternity specialist expressed two items of concern. They found a cyst in Beckham's brain, which some doctors believed to be a normal part of development. It could either dissolve naturally or prove fatal. Second, the umbilical cord insertion was to the side, not the middle, of the placenta. This could slow the growth rate of the baby. At thirty weeks, another sonogram revealed that the cyst was gone, and our baby was growing normally. We were relieved but knew from experience that delivery day could bring difficult surprises.

That takes us back to the day of Beckham's sonogram. The room was crowded with grandparents, aunts, uncles, and cousins. Tears welled up as we saw our son flash us the okay sign. In that moment, the anxiety lifted, and I started to believe everything would truly be okay. And sure enough, when we welcomed our son in August, it was.

# A BLAST

*I'm fun. Not just mildly amusing. Huge fun! When I come, I'm gonna help you do things you haven't done since you were young. We're going to make memories. Have a grand time. We can play and laugh at nothing or everything. Hard, big, belly, nose-snorting laughs. Won't we have fun in the sun or sometimes when I wake up in the middle of the night? To me, tiny toes are funny. Big chins make me grin. See? It's gonna be a blast.*

## BABY NOTES

What do you want your child to know for certain? What are you looking forward to teaching him? Or experiencing with her?

.........................................................................

.........................................................................

.........................................................................

.........................................................................

.........................................................................

.........................................................................

.........................................................................

.........................................................................

.........................................................................

# week *EIGHTEEN*

You may be feeling baby flutters

# week EIGHTEEN

*It is the sweet, simple things of life which are the real ones after all.*
—LAURA INGALLS WILDER

**I'M THIS BIG:** I'm eight inches long, and I weigh six ounces.

www.tyndal.es/twwyweek18

This baby seems to be waving at her parents, who just discovered that she's a girl. Notice the detail in her fingers and how the umbilical cord falls over her face. You can also clearly see facial features like her lips and her pert little nose. Baby is also able to show some expression, so don't be surprised if a sonogram shows baby squint, suck, or grimace.

# DEVELOPMENT

By week eighteen, you might be able to feel me move. My taste buds cover the inside of the mouth.[1] My eyes may be sensitive to bright light.[2] My ears are standing out from my head. I get my oxygen from you through the placenta. My heart is probably beating about 130 to 150 beats a minute.

# Rx FOR HEALTH

The umbilical cord may end up around baby's neck. This condition, called a nuchal cord, is a common occurrence and usually doesn't result in harm. It can be seen on ultrasound, but most of the time it's an incidental finding at the time of delivery. However, a nuchal cord can make a baby less tolerant of labor and result in the need for C-section.

Pregnancy can come with an increased risk for dental problems. Increases in progesterone levels can cause minor issues like bad breath to major problems such as gum disease. Be sure to brush regularly and drink water after your meals. See a dentist at least once during your pregnancy.

**NUTRITIONAL NUGGET**
You need about three hundred more healthy calories a day starting in your second trimester. You should probably gain about ten pounds during your first twenty weeks, and about one pound per week after that. But most of the twenty-five to thirty-five pounds you're supposed to gain truly are baby weight. Here's an approximate breakdown of where those pounds go:[3]

- Baby—eight pounds
- Breast size—two to three pounds
- Placenta—two to three pounds
- Amniotic fluid—two to three pounds
- Increased blood volume—four pounds
- Fat stores—five to nine pounds
- Uterus growth—two to five pounds

## MOMMY MOMENTS

### "You Move Me"

It's hard to forget the first time your baby gives you a swift kick. Call it a milestone . . . for us, not for them. They've been kicking it up for months.

*The first time I felt a kick, I was standing in front of the kitchen sink, and I had the odd sensation that something on the counter tapped me. It took me a few seconds to realize what had happened.* —LINDA ROY

*When I first felt my daughter move, I was anchoring the weekend news. I wanted to tell all of Kansas City on the air!* —KIM BYRNES

*I was sitting at my desk at work when I felt a flutter in my stomach. I froze and it happened again, and I knew I'd just felt my baby kick.* —RENEÉ VELA

*I was eighteen weeks along when I first felt my son move. It felt like a butterfly.* —JENNIFER WICKERSHAM

*I was in my bed, lying on my stomach, and I felt a little jump like a fish flipping over. I screamed for my husband to come and touch my belly, but he couldn't feel anything.* —AMANDA CHAPMAN

# PRENATAL POSTCARD

## She Did It Again by Brandy Bruce

she did it again. I opened my eyes. A neon light from the bed stand told me it was a little after four in the morning. I groaned and somehow managed to roll myself into a sitting position. By my eighth month of pregnancy, sleep had become a luxury that kept escaping me. My active baby girl was pretending to be a soccer player at her favorite time of day—any time after midnight. Throughout my pregnancy, from the first time I felt Ashtyn kick, she seemed to be most active during the hours I desperately needed rest.

Honestly, I had no idea how difficult sleeping would be! It makes sense, of course. It's hard to get comfortable when there's a basketball everywhere you turn. But as any pregnant woman will tell you, the irony is that even though you're utterly exhausted, you can't sleep.

So I sat at the edge of the bed, rubbing my big belly while my husband slept soundly. Another kick to the ribs reminded me that Ashtyn was with me. But as tired as I felt, her kicks could never cause that much frustration. They were this amazing reminder that a little person was growing inside of me, that she was part of me. As had become my routine, I began praying for Ashtyn, for her health and her future. I prayed that I would be a good mother. Once the kicking subsided (temporarily), I crawled back into my semicomfortable sleeping position.

Now that Ashtyn is bouncing around the house and practicing her ABCs, I think back on those middle-of-the-night kicks and prayers. The truth is that I wouldn't trade those moments for anything.

# "DID YOU FEEL THAT?"

*Flutter. Sputter. Putter. Pinch. Poke. Punch. Did you feel that bump? I think I felt you jump. Finally. It's me! I've been trying to make you see. And feel. It's not a butterfly or gas or a tummy rumble. It's my twist and my kick and my double-flip tumble.*

*Are my muscles and bones finally strong enough to reach you? Beat you? Hello there, Mama! I'm just trying to greet you.*

## BABY NOTES

Have you felt your baby kick yet? If so, describe when, where, and how often.

.................................................................................................

.................................................................................................

.................................................................................................

.................................................................................................

.................................................................................................

.................................................................................................

.................................................................................................

.................................................................................................

.................................................................................................

.................................................................................................

# week
# NINETEEN

It's time for the big reveal
(if you want!)

# week NINETEEN

I'M THIS BIG: I'm eight and a half inches long, and I weigh seven ounces.

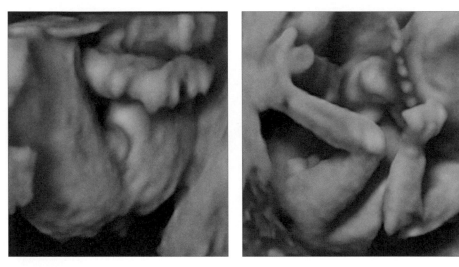

www.tyndal.es/twwyweek19

It's time for the big reveal. If you want to find out whether a he or a she is growing inside you, you probably can now. Here's an example: in the first image, you can see the labia of a baby girl. The baby on the right is a curled-up little man. The cord ripples in front of his face.

# DEVELOPMENT

At nineteen weeks, my boy or girl parts are apparent on a sonogram. My nervous system is complete. I can hear your heart pumping and your stomach rumbling. My fingers, legs, and wrists can bend and flex. I can spin circles and do somersaults.

# RX FOR HEALTH

Usually health-care providers order a diagnostic sonogram between eighteen and twenty-two weeks of pregnancy to check on baby's organ function and growth. All of baby's parts are big enough to see clearly on a sonogram. We can look closely at the brain, heart, and spine. If there are any abnormalities, further testing may be recommended. This is important for baby because in some situations, we would have an opportunity to intervene medically, if necessary.

**NUTRITIONAL NUGGET**
Vitamin D helps with the formation of baby's bones and is necessary for tissue growth. It's also associated with higher birth weights among babies. Many women have vitamin D deficiencies, especially vegetarians. The main source of vitamin D is sunlight, absorbed through our skin. Interestingly, exposure to sunlight during winter months when the rays are weaker produces little or no vitamin D in your body. Because exposure to sunlight varies depending on where you live, it's important to drink milk fortified with vitamin D. Other sources include fish and eggs. The amount currently recommended for pregnant women is 600 IU.[1]

# Mommy Moments

## From the Inside Out

Are you having a boy or a girl? Our pregnant maternal ancestors would have had to wait about four more months to find out. Some mothers want it to be a surprise, but for others, this is a defining moment in their pregnancies and their lives! If you're going to take a peek in advance, plan to celebrate!

*When the doctor said our baby had a third leg, my husband didn't get her joke. He was getting concerned over the third leg until she announced that it was our baby's penis. After that you could have told my husband that the baby had three arms and a head the size of a melon. All he thought about from that moment on was,* I'm having a son. —Heather England

*With Izabella, I was elated, and my husband was in shock. In the sonogram photo, she was "spread eagle," so there was no mistaking the gender.* —Kristin Morris

*We didn't find out with Evan until he was born. That was wonderful! We chose to find out in a sonogram with Claire, but we kept it a secret from our whole family and didn't even tell them until years later that we had known.* —Jana Calkins

*I've been pregnant five times, and we've never found out beforehand what we were having. I clearly remember the birth of our second baby. One of the sweetest memories in life was hearing my husband announce, "It's a boy!" in the delivery room. I can still clearly hear his voice with all the emotion as if it were happening right now.* —Anette Gettinger

112

# Prenatal Postcard

## Mother's Intuition Gone Awry
## by Lucy Weber

I am a planner. The question was never if we would find out the sex of our baby but how soon could we find out? With our first, the sonographer pointed to the relevant area and said, "Look, it's a boy." We nodded. It was obvious even to us.

During my second pregnancy, it was different. We were told, "It's a girl!" Squinting toward the fuzzy, gray shapes on the screen, I said, "Really?" I was not convinced! I didn't know what I was looking at and was pretty sure the doctor had made a mistake. I felt exactly the same as my first pregnancy. I had heard so many people say that pregnancies are different with boys and girls. So I had a few extra sonograms. Two more professionals ruled: a girl! Finally I bought some girl clothes but kept all the tags on and double-checked the stores' return policies.

On the way to the hospital, I made sure my husband knew where all the blue bedding and clothing were stored so he could change out the nursery if necessary. The moment came, the baby was born, and I asked, "What is it?"

My midwife said, "It's a girl. I thought you knew that!"

It's a good thing I'd saved all those tags and receipts! And wow, what a girl she is! As if to firmly stamp her place in this family, she is a pink-loving, fashionable, caring, nurturing, sparkly princess.

## "A WINDOW TO MY WORLD"

*You look at me with that thing on your tummy. You're happy to see me. It's true. I wish you knew all the things I can do. It will take just a second to show you a few. I can wiggle really well. Move my knees to my hips. I can squint. I can yawn. I can pucker my lips. You're impressed. Don't I know! I'm quite the little miss—or mister. The sonographer can look, you can see too, unless you decide not to peek till I'm through.*

## BABY NOTES

Describe your ultrasound experience. Do you want to know your baby's gender? Why or why not?

.............................................................................................

.............................................................................................

.............................................................................................

.............................................................................................

.............................................................................................

.............................................................................................

.............................................................................................

.............................................................................................

.............................................................................................

# week
# TWENTY

Some of your baby's teeth are
forming in the jawbone

# week TWENTY

I'M THIS BIG: I'm nine and a half inches long, and I weigh twelve ounces.

www.tyndal.es/twwyweek20

Look at this sweet baby raise his or her little fist to the mouth. The facial expression is so serious, but the babe is probably sleeping. Baby is halfway through his or her time in the womb and is already forming distinct facial features.

# Development

By week twenty, I have some teeth forming in my jawbone. My skin is coated with vernix, a creamy, thick substance that adheres to the light hair on my body and protects my skin from the amniotic fluid. My heart is beating about 120 to 160 times a minute. You can almost certainly feel me moving by now. Doctors call it "quickening."

# Rx for Health

You might wonder whether ultrasound is safe during pregnancy. Ultrasound consists of sound waves, not radiation, and no credible studies have shown that exposure to ultrasound is harmful to baby. Numerous conditions require frequent monitoring of baby's well-being by ultrasound.

**NUTRITIONAL NUGGET**
Alcohol in any amount is never recommended for pregnant women because there is no known safe level of alcohol consumption during pregnancy. Studies show that even two drinks a day can adversely affect babies, lowering their IQs after birth.[1] According to the American College of Obstetricians and Gynecologists, alcohol is a leading cause of mental retardation in babies.[2] When you take a drink, so does your baby. The same amount of alcohol in Mom's blood finds its way to baby's blood, and baby's liver isn't able to break it down. A mother's heavy drinking may cause fetal alcohol syndrome.

**DID YOU KNOW?**
Researchers discovered that from eighteen weeks on, a baby can distinguish light outside the womb. When a direct light was shined on a mother's stomach, the baby usually looked the other way. The baby's heart rate also reacts when light is shined on the mother's stomach.[3]

# MOMMY MOMENTS

## Imagining Baby

We can't help but wonder what our little one will look like. Curly hair or straight? Brunette or redhead? Will he be rowdy or calm? A sports star or a bookworm? Princess or tomboy? We try to guess based on activity levels and habits that baby may reveal now. Sometimes we're spot on, but there will always be surprises.

*Logan isn't at all like I thought he'd be. He moved very little while I was pregnant. Now he can't sit still. He runs and hops everywhere.*
—LAURISA MYERS

*My baby kicked constantly. I always said, "This baby is gonna be a mover and shaker and one heck of a dancer." Guess what? I was right! When she turned three, we enrolled her in dance class.* —KIM BYRNES

*Connor kicked mostly at night when I was trying to relax, which is just like him now. He doesn't ever want to go to bed.* —TRACY MCMINN

*I slept great during my first pregnancy and never had any pain. Even now, my son is very calm and a great sleeper. I'm pregnant now with boy number two, and he is totally different. He kicks hard enough to wake me up. I'm a little anxious to see if I will ever sleep again.* —HEIDI WICKERSHAM

# PRENATAL POSTCARD

## Great Expectations by Andrea Hougland

Our first surprise came one warm August evening. Just four months after our picture-perfect wedding, two lines stared up at me from a hurriedly purchased home pregnancy test. Disbelieving, the control freak in me took another test . . . and then another. The shock shifted to a mild sense of fear . . . and finally joy. Then the dreams started. I had my first taste of mother's intuition, and it was screaming, "Boy!"

Halfway through my pregnancy, our sonographer quickly determined our baby's sex and sealed the secret in an envelope. She assured us she hadn't been wrong in twenty years. We wanted to share the mystery with our family, so I took the envelope to a party store. Behind my back, the clerks filled a box with balloons. That night with family gathered round, my husband and I lifted the lid. Pink balloons floated heavenward along with the cheers of our entire family. My second surprise. I'd felt sure we were having a boy.

My loved ones held four pretty pink baby showers doused in roses and ribbon. We dolled up the nursery and hung a banner over the crib to welcome Baby Avery home.

Both families came to the hospital and listened outside the delivery room door on delivery day. As soon as our baby's first cry seeped into the hallway, they started calling and texting everyone, announcing Avery's arrival to the world.

On the other side of those doors, surprise number three had just entered my well-ordered life. My husband gazed down at our new bundle of joy dumbfounded. "Honey, it's a boy." The doctor hoisted him up and said "Congratulations!" Wide-eyed, I stared at my baby's boy parts . . . just to make sure. My mother's intuition just trumped the twenty-first-century medical tests. And then we made a lot of returns and exchanges. Maternal love made an immediate mental transition. And then we made a lot of returns and exchanges.

# "EW, THE GOO!"

*I'm minding my own business in here, when suddenly . . . it appears. It's slimy and squishy, soft and mushy. It starts on my back and then on my arms and legs. It feels like—it looks like—well, kind of like eggs. Not hard-boiled or soft-boiled. It's a little like honey, but not so runny. It's all over my tummy. It's some kind of lotion potion, protecting my skin. I hope it comes off before I meet my kin!*

## BABY NOTES

Based on your baby's activity in the womb, what do you think he or she will be like?

.......................................................................

.......................................................................

.......................................................................

.......................................................................

.......................................................................

.......................................................................

.......................................................................

.......................................................................

.......................................................................

# week TWENTY-ONE

You and baby are more than halfway there!

# week TWENTY-ONE

I'M THIS BIG: I'm ten inches long, and I weigh almost one pound.

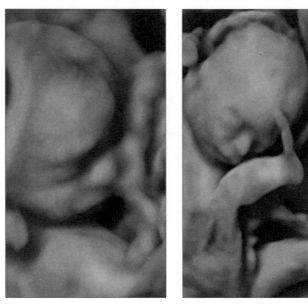

www.tyndal.es/twwyweek21

These are two images of the same baby. In the close-up on the left, you can see the cord pushed against baby's tiny profile. On the right, this little boy is proving that he may be a good NFL draft pick as a kicker someday. In that image, the umbilical cord is coiled over his head like a tiny halo. At this point, babies still have quite a bit of room in the uterus for movement. That means the cord may frequently be wrapped around body parts. At this stage in pregnancy, the cord usually corrects itself.

*All that I am, or hope to be,*
*I owe to my angel mother.*
*—ABRAHAM LINCOLN*

# DEVELOPMENT

At twenty-one weeks, I swallow amniotic fluid. My digestive system is starting to work. If you can find it by yourself, you might be able to hear my heartbeat with a stethoscope. The number of cells in my brain is increasing, and my hair is growing.

# RX FOR HEALTH

At twenty weeks, most health-care providers will begin measuring baby's growth from outside the womb using a tape measure. Between twenty and thirty-four weeks, the fundal height (the measurement from the mother's pubic bone to the top of the uterus in centimeters) is the same as the gestational age of the baby. Even though all moms carry babies differently, their fundal heights are roughly the same during this period. If the fundal height deviates significantly from the gestational age, your provider will most likely order an ultrasound.

**NUTRITIONAL NUGGET**
When you're pregnant, smoking is not only bad for you; it's hazardous for your baby. When a mother smokes, it robs oxygen and food from her baby. The result is sometimes miscarriage, stillbirth, placental bleeding, or low birthweight.

**DID YOU KNOW?**
Grasping reflexes have now developed, allowing baby to hold his or her own hands, feet, or even the umbilical cord. Sonographers have even seen identical twins in the same sac reach out and grab each other.

## MOMMY MOMENTS
### My Best Gift

Blankets, bottles, clothes, and diapers for baby. A massage, body pillow, and pedicure for Mom. Gifts of any kind are a blessing when you're preparing to bring a new baby home. While some presents are practical, others are priceless!

*At my baby shower, my mom gave me a box of dresses that I wore when I was a baby, along with a picture of me in them! Needless to say, I shed a few tears when I opened that present.* —KRISTIN MORRIS

*I worked at a school, and one of the classes got together and gave me a huge basket of books for all ages, some of which we're just getting around to reading now, seven years later.* —LUCY WEBER

*Kenya, where I'm from, is a very communal society. When you're pregnant, you're surrounded, and there's usually a naming ceremony where you announce the baby's name and receive gifts and feast. Pregnant for the first time in the States with my husband, I missed my culture and my family. So I really appreciated the showers people gave me. Also, receiving notes and texts and gifts from all over the world made me feel loved and encouraged.* —NANCY YOUREE

*My neighbors gave me a beautiful bouquet of roses and a soft baby blanket for my son. That blanket ended up going to bed with him every night for eight years!* —CORY GUISLER

124

# Prenatal Postcard

## An Unexpected Gift by Anne Reade

It was the most difficult phone call I've ever had to make. I was eighteen years old and four months pregnant. It was time to tell my parents.

Raised in a strict home, I went a little wild during my first year away at college. I drank, partied, and secretly dated a guy my parents didn't like. Maybe for good reason. He did drugs and hated God.

As I dialed my parents' phone number, my thoughts flew back to the day I found out. I was almost through my first trimester when the pregnancy test read positive. Shocked and afraid, I began to cry. My boyfriend, Brandon, and I went to Planned Parenthood to get a sonogram. We saw the little heart beating on the screen. I knew I was keeping this baby.

When my parents picked up the phone, I told them I was pregnant. My fears were realized. They were furious. My dad called Brandon and then his parents. Dad's knee-jerk reaction was to protect me. He wanted me to quit school and come home.

As a baby, I was adopted. My parents encouraged me to make the same decision my birth mother had made at age fifteen. I couldn't. Brandon wouldn't.

My parents eventually calmed down and became supportive. I stayed in school. We all saw a counselor who helped us cope and taught me how to be a mother. I immediately quit drinking. My grades improved. I found a church and started reading my Bible again. Slowly Brandon's heart also began to change.

Physically, my pregnancy was uncomplicated. Emotionally, it was very painful. I was hurled headlong into adulthood.

I will never regret my decision to keep Nora Ann. She is a gift from God that forced me to change. My decisions, my grades, my circumstances all improved. She saved Brandon even more. If not for her, he would probably be in prison, or dead. Instead, he has become a believer and a good father. God's best gifts sometimes come in very unexpected packages.

# HALFTIME

*Are we almost there? What's that you say? Only halfway? This is quite a long trip.*
*Did we pack enough stuff? Did we bring enough food? I wonder when I'll get my*
*first pair of shoes. I've been staring at these toes for twenty-one weekers. They sure*
*would look nice in a new pair of sneakers. Nineteen more weeks to go . . . 133 days.*
*That's a lifetime away . . . like January to May. I wish my due date was today!*

## BABY NOTES

You're halfway there! What still needs to be done before you're ready to bring baby home?

...........................................................................

...........................................................................

...........................................................................

...........................................................................

...........................................................................

...........................................................................

...........................................................................

...........................................................................

...........................................................................

# week TWENTY-TWO

Baby has fingernails and can taste sweet and bitter flavors

# week TWENTY-TWO

**I'M THIS BIG:** I'm ten and a half inches long, and I weigh one pound.

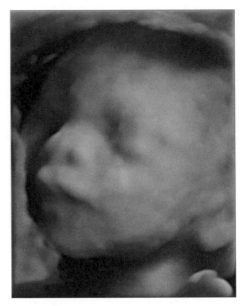

www.tyndal.es/twwyweek22

This baby is tilting his chin upward, snuggling into Mom's uterus. Look at the beautiful lips and earlobe. In the next few weeks, baby will be able to distinguish sounds outside the womb. Studies have shown that babies in utero move and kick in rhythm to music their mothers are listening to. If the music and beat are loud, baby moves quickly. When slow classical music plays, baby calms down.

# Development

My fingernails began growing weeks ago, and now, at twenty-two weeks, they cover my whole nail bed. I can control my movements now. I can hold on to the umbilical cord. I can taste sweet and bitter flavors. My inner ear is fully developed. Hair on my head and body (called lanugo) is present.

# Rx for Health

Many medications may be necessary for a mom during her pregnancy. It's always important to discuss risks versus benefits with your health-care provider. Pregnant women absorb and metabolize medications differently than nonpregnant women. Extensive research has been conducted on the use of certain antidepressants during pregnancy and lactation, as well the effects of untreated depression on a pregnancy. Recent studies indicate that some psychiatric medications can and should be used safely when indicated, but women should talk with their physician first about risks and benefits.[1]

**NUTRITIONAL NUGGET**
If you're lactose intolerant, you have to work hard to get enough calcium and vitamin D during pregnancy. Milk is a nutrient-dense food that is hard to replace in the diet. You may try calcium-rich vegetables, fortified soy milk, or yogurt. Supplements containing 600 mg of calcium and 200 IU of vitamin D may be the best alternative if you're allergic to all dairy products.

## MOMMY MOMENTS

### A Matter of Taste

Babies' taste buds pop out during the first trimester. They multiply throughout gestation and become more refined from birth to toddlerhood. So what you're eating now, baby is also enjoying . . . or not. Beware. Those picky preferences are likely to live on.

*I ate BLT sandwiches twice a day while I was pregnant. Now Bella loves bacon.* —KIM BYRNES

*I love chocolate, but when I was pregnant, it made me sick. Now Brandi still doesn't like chocolate.* —ROBERTA SIMPSON

*We realized when I was pregnant that Peyton didn't like shrimp. I was never sick throughout my entire pregnancy except for when I ate shrimp. My son still hates shrimp, and I have become allergic to it.* —REBECCA KOENEKE

*I craved Mexican food during my second pregnancy. Now my daughter Jordan has no problem eating hot stuff!* —JENNIFER RODRIGUEZ

*I craved dill pickles and all three of my kids love them now!*
—DANIELLE GOOD

# PRENATAL POSTCARD

## Hummus Among Us by Lynne Carols

I'm not a big meat eater, so in an effort to add some protein to my pregnancy diet, I discovered hummus. And I dove in. Like a double backflip off a Mediterranean cliff. Garlic hummus on crackers. Sun-dried tomato hummus with veggies. Southwest hummus on toast, bagels, and wraps.

Then along came my baby boy. Breastfed on milk that was decidedly laced with a dash of maternal love and, you guessed it, more hummus.

By the time my son was about eight months old, I was attempting to make my own organic baby food. Problem was, my guy wouldn't eat half of it. He refused the farm-grown kale I steamed and blended so he could be a superbaby. He snubbed almost anything green. Clamped his baby lips closed and turned his head to the wall. Until what I call my "chickpea epiphany."

I was snacking on hummus and something, and he was sitting in his high chair snubbing my pureed produce and staring enviously at my hummus! I followed his eyes to my obsession on the table, grabbed his baby spoon, and mixed a dollop into his dark-green kale.

He opened his mouth wide like a baby bird beggin' for worms! Eureka! From then on, I mixed hummus with everything on his plate. I don't want to admit to the combinations he would inhale as long as the recipe included hummus. As my baby became a toddler, he learned to make hummus with me. He would go to the fridge and start pulling out the tahini and lemon juice and other ingredients most toddler fingers have never touched. He would scoot the kitchen chair up to the counter and exclaim, "It's hummus time!" And I would gladly comply, finally realizing it was in his blood . . . or at least in his amniotic fluid . . . long before birth.

(For Lynne's favorite hummus recipe, go to www.thewonderwithinyou.com.)

## "WHAT'S IT LIKE?"

*I was wondering in here, what's it like out there? What's a kite? Can we fly one? A red cherry Popsicle? I'd sure like to try one. Can we go outside and catch bugs? What's air? I need a hug. Does Daddy have hair? What's light? And night? And who wants to sleep? And when do we play? Can I have a puppy to keep? Do I have a brother or sister? Do I get one? When? Don't answer that yet; I'll ask you again.*

## BABY NOTES

As a mom, how do you most want to be like your mother? How do you want to be different?

........................................................................

........................................................................

........................................................................

........................................................................

........................................................................

........................................................................

........................................................................

........................................................................

........................................................................

# week TWENTY-THREE

By this week, your baby can hear sounds

# week TWENTY-THREE

**I'M THIS BIG:** I'm eleven inches long, and I weigh just over one pound.

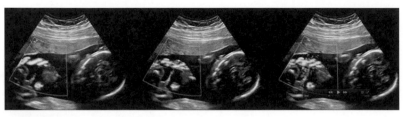

www.tyndal.es/twwyweek23

Your baby is now able to urinate inside the womb. That means the digestive system is beginning to do its job. Sometimes you might see this in Doppler during a sonogram. In these images, the newly announced baby boy has just proved to his parents that he's male. Look on the left inside the green boxes. It looks like a Roman candle with a flare streaming proudly as baby relieves himself. (See the video at www.thewonderwithinyou.com.)

## DEVELOPMENT

By week twenty-three, I may hear some sounds outside your uterus. My skin is red and wrinkled. I'm continuing to put on a little fat. Meconium is collecting in my intestines. It's a waste product that wasn't transferred back to you through the placenta. It is sticky and blackish-green in color and will turn into my first poop . . . hopefully not until after delivery.

134

# Rx for Health

Many moms are concerned about safety during pregnancy. Here is a list of what's considered safe and unsafe based on some most-asked questions on the topic:

**SAFE**

- Using a microwave—No solid studies show any adverse effects.
- Using an electric blanket—It's probably safest on low settings; however, most pregnant women are naturally hot and won't need it.
- Riding in a plane—In a normal pregnancy, it's safe to fly until thirty-four weeks; in a high-risk pregnancy, you may need to stop sooner.
- Coloring hair—A lot of health-care providers will encourage you to avoid using color in the first trimester, since there aren't convincing studies one way or another on safety.
- Drinking diet soda—Aim for moderation—one or two sodas, coffees, or teas a day.

**UNSAFE**

- Tanning beds—Research on this isn't great, but since tanning isn't necessary and isn't considered healthy for women generally speaking, it's discouraged.
- Secondhand smoke—Not much literature exists on the effects of secondhand smoke on pregnant women, but it's safe to assume it may carry the same risks as smoking.

**NUTRITIONAL NUGGET**
Most pregnant women shouldn't restrict their salt intake. Your desire for salty foods may increase during pregnancy. This is a normal change. Pregnant women require a bit more sodium. Extreme salt restriction may actually be harmful. Although pregnant women shouldn't eat salt to excess, it can be consumed "to taste." Women with preexisting hypertension should work closely with their health-care providers to control their blood pressure during and after pregnancy.

135

# Mommy Moments

## "Do You Hear What I Hear?"

Although baby's hearing will improve as your pregnancy goes on, studies show that baby can hear at twenty-three weeks. Moms can tell without the studies, because babies just have a way of letting us know.

*My mom was having hardwood floors put in her new house, and every time they used the air gun to push the boards together, Hannah would kick or jump!* —Kelly Carpenter

*I played music to both babies. Dylan didn't have a huge reaction; Kelsy would kick and move. I could tell she loved it. They both are music fans now and love to sing and dance.* —Karla Shotts

*I talked to my baby all the time. I read* Goodnight Moon *and* Big Red Barn*. I know he recognized my voice because the day he was born, he cried while the nurses worked on me. When I finally got to hold and talk to him, he stopped crying and listened and snuggled up to me. Tears of joy, still to this day.* —Chris Barcus

*When I was pregnant with my daughter, she was so sweet that when I'd ask if she was okay in there, she almost always would give me a kick in response!* —June Santiago

136

# PRENATAL POSTCARD

## Our Song by Noreen Dupriest

During my pregnancy, I often sang a sorority song while I rubbed my growing belly. Always the same song, same tune, same words. My pregnancy developed beautifully until contractions started at thirty-four weeks. Unaware that my placenta had begun to separate from my uterus, I quickly and tumultuously delivered our baby. He was in neonatal intensive care for a week. I adored little Preston. During that first week, I went to the hospital every three hours to feed him. Between the curtains we hid. He nursed, and I sang our song. He nestled into my arms, and it soothed him.

As the days passed, my son grew stronger and was released from the hospital. Our song remained part of our daily routine. It was a bonding time we both desperately needed. My sweet baby soon became a toddler. His knobby knees would sometimes give out. One day after a tumble, I started to sing our song. Almost immediately his sadness disappeared. He looked at me with absolute peace. The words I began singing before he was born were as powerful as a kiss.

My baby is now nine. He still sometimes asks me to sing "my" song. Afterward he says to me, "Mommy, you have the most beautiful voice."

# JUST RIGHT

*No matter what I'm like, I'll be just right for you. I may be quick to smile or slow to talk. Suck my thumb. Wobble when I walk. Motormouth. Cry and pout. Busy body. Slow to train on the potty. I might like to play patty-cake or push the peas right off my plate . . . onto the floor. And then ask for more. What if I can't hit the ball with my bat? Or if my teacher says I'm no good at math? Mom, can't you see, no matter what type I'm like, you'll love me instantly 'cause I'm made just right!*

## BABY NOTES

How are you feeling at this point in your pregnancy?

.................................................................................

.................................................................................

.................................................................................

.................................................................................

.................................................................................

.................................................................................

.................................................................................

.................................................................................

.................................................................................

# week TWENTY-FOUR

### Space is getting tighter in your uterus

# week TWENTY-FOUR

## I'M THIS BIG: I'm twelve inches long, and I weigh 1.3 pounds.

www.tyndal.es/twwyweek24

*A mother understands what a baby does not say.*
—JEWISH PROVERB

You've come a long way, baby! Just to let you know how far we've come in one generation, think about this: This little guy's mama is an identical twin, born in 1980. Her mom never had an ultrasound or X-ray during pregnancy. On delivery day, she was knocked out during a C-section and woke up with surprise twins. That almost never happens today. In fact, the little twin born a surprise has now seen her twenty-four-week-old baby in three separate ultrasounds. She knows not only his sex but also what his face looks like. And she has already witnessed some of his sweet mannerisms.

# Development

By week twenty-four, you may see your stomach move when I kick and turn. Space is getting tighter in your uterus. I'm getting longer. I have creases on my hands, fingers, and toes. My skin is wrinkled and red or pink in color.

# Rx for Health

Some women begin having contractions very early in their pregnancies. Although baby might be able to live outside the uterus at this point, the goal is to continue the pregnancy as long as possible. If you begin to experience contractions, contact your health-care provider immediately. He or she will assess whether intervention is needed.

Braxton Hicks contractions can begin as early as the second trimester. They differ from labor contractions in that they are not painful and they do not tend to come with any regularity. Braxton Hicks contractions tend to be shorter in length than labor contractions and do not result in changing of the cervix.

**NUTRITIONAL NUGGET**
Food-borne illnesses are never good, but they can be especially harmful during pregnancy. Certain bacteria found in foods can hurt the baby and cause miscarriage, premature birth, or stillbirth. High levels of mercury in some fish may pass through the placenta to baby. (We will talk more about the benefits and dangers of fish during week twenty-seven.)

It's best not to eat the following:

- Improperly canned food
- Undercooked meat
- Raw or undercooked eggs
- Soft cheese like feta, brie, Camembert, queso blanco, and queso fresco
- Unpasteurized milk or fruit juices
- Sushi
- King mackerel
- Tilefish
- Shark
- Swordfish

**DID YOU KNOW?**
Baby's movements are most frequent around the middle of your pregnancy. They slow down as space gets more limited. Busy babies are building strong muscles and bones.

# MOMMY MOMENTS

## Kickin' It with Mom

Most babies establish habits of wake and sleep time. If you pay attention, you might be able to discover more about those habits or notice patterns. They may be similar after baby is born.

*My baby was always quiet and sleepy in the mornings and wide awake and kicking late at night. After he was born, he continued the same pattern till he was almost two months old.* —THEA BLEDSOE CLAP

*I noticed really early on that Miss Emma loved late-evening dance parties. She could always be counted on to wiggle and squirm the most between 10:00 p.m. and midnight, when I was trying to go to sleep. She's three months old now and is just starting to not be such a night owl.* —JENNIFER HUCKABY

*When I was pregnant with my son Brody, he always seemed to kick after breakfast. Even now I can remember that little foot, digging into my side. Those are precious memories for me.* —JULIA ASHWORTH

*When I was pregnant with Annie, she regularly kicked most of the night but then slept soundly from about 6:00 to 11:00 a.m. This was perfect for me as I'm a night owl and liked to sleep late. Even now, at ten months of age, she sleeps much later in the morning than most babies her age!* —SARAH GRAY

# PRENATAL POSTCARD

## Just Wondering . . . by Mary Pulley

It never fails! Each night I finally clear my head and find a comfy spot lodged between Randall and my maternity pillow. My eyes close, my head relaxes, and my body goes limp . . . and then I feel it. A sudden and very distinctive kick from Landen! It has wakened me from my deepest sleep.

My first thought is always, Are you okay in there? I can't help but wonder if I'm squishing him. Sometimes when I bend down to get something, I feel his sudden movements. Of course my imagination goes crazy, and that's never a good thing! Where's his head? Did I wake him? Did I startle him?

Then I frantically Google everything from "how to sit when you're pregnant" to "how many times your baby should move in a day." I try not to obsess.

I've been looking for patterns. He usually gets me up in the morning with a kick to the ribs. I usually feel him again after breakfast and lunch. The funniest thing to me is that whenever I listen to live music or start typing, he begins to move! Then of course he moves the most at night while I'm trying to wind down, and again once I'm asleep. That's his norm, but there are some days when I feel like he's not moving very much at all. So then I play loud music, jiggle my belly, or eat something spicy . . . and he still won't budge. It makes me frantic!

Then when I'm least expecting it, I get a football kick to my navel, making my whole belly move! Even though it's not the most pleasant feeling, especially considering I drink a lot of water, it has become incredibly comforting. It's like his way of saying, "Mom, chill out! I'm okay. I'm just doing what the unborn do."

# "I LIKE TO KICK"

*I like to kick . . . especially at night. Just when you start to settle down, I gear up. Do I have your full attention now? Pow! I give you a punch and then a wiggle, a knee, and a turn. When I roll over, do you see your whole belly churn? That's funny. Isn't it great when I kick you at night? Just to let you know everything's all right.*

## BABY NOTES

What time of day is your baby most active? Are you getting enough rest these days?

.................................................................................

.................................................................................

.................................................................................

.................................................................................

.................................................................................

.................................................................................

.................................................................................

.................................................................................

.................................................................................

# week
# TWENTY-
# FIVE

Baby can open his or her eyes
and sense changes in light

# week TWENTY-FIVE

### I'M THIS BIG: I'm twelve and a half inches long, and I weigh one and a half pounds.

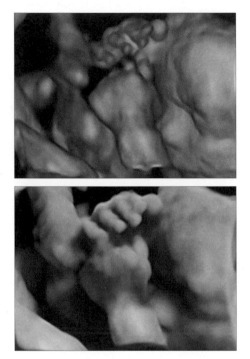

www.tyndal.es/twwyweek25

Look at the difference in these two images. The one above was obtained using the traditional 3-D ultrasound technique. The second image was captured using GE's new high-definition equipment. Notice the difference in color, light, and definition. It almost looks like a photograph. Who knows how we'll see early life when these babies are having babies?

Look at this baby's fingers gently resting on the swirl of the umbilical cord. One hand is open; the other is curled into a loose fist. The facial features are stunning. Doesn't this make you want to go kiss a baby?

*Children are likely to live up to what you believe of them.*
—LADY BIRD JOHNSON

# Development

At twenty-five weeks, I can open my eyes and sense changes in light. My lungs are developing, and I'm starting to make breathing movements. My sweat glands are forming. I can feel when something touches me.

# Rx for Health

Every mom has aches and pains during pregnancy. Most are normal, but a few may need to be checked out. Sudden shortness of breath or difficulty breathing could be a sign of a blood clot in the lung. Abdominal pain, changes in your vision, or a decrease in your baby's movements are other symptoms that would warrant calling your health-care provider. This doesn't always mean something is wrong, but it's better to be safe than sorry. Whenever something doesn't feel right, it's important to talk to your provider.

**NUTRITIONAL NUGGET**
Only a few medications have been proven safe to take during pregnancy. Many herbal remedies aren't adequately tested for safety in pregnant women, and only a handful of prescription medications are considered absolutely safe. Consult your health-care provider before taking medication or herbal supplements. He or she usually has a current list of what is safe.

# MOMMY MOMENTS

## Feathering the Nest

Like a bird before she lays her eggs, human moms have a natural nesting instinct. It's a pregnancy rite of passage. It often occurs during the frantic homestretch to baby day. Physically it can wear you out, but mentally it usually makes mamas feel a whole lot better.

*Months seven and eight, I was organizing and reorganizing. It's a good thing, because I was too tired by month nine!* —MARINA MCFARREN

*My nesting goes into full swing during early contractions. With my first two babies, I was vacuuming the entire house and taking breaks for especially strong contractions. My husband thought I was crazy! With my third, I didn't even unpack baby clothing or do final nursery decorations until I started contractions. They lasted all day long, and I organized baby clothing in between contractions. Talk about waiting until the last moment!* —HEIDI MAGGIO

*When I started cleaning the oven and cleaning floors on my hands and knees, we knew baby was coming soon!* —MICHELLE ALLEN

*I went into crazy nesting mode with each pregnancy. I think I drove my husband mad with all the honey-do's I gave him!* —JENNY OJALA

# Prenatal Postcard

## Turbo Nesting by Jeanene Kiesling

The previous year of my life had been nothing short of crazy. I unexpectedly lost my mom and best friend after short, fierce battles with cancer. Months later I got married. A few months after that, I was pregnant. My husband and I were overjoyed and a bit overwhelmed.

We had just moved into a beautiful new house, but our unpredictable work hours meant we would soon need a nanny. Financially something had to give. So we did something I never thought I would do. We moved into the home where I grew up.

The old home needed massive renovation. We had ten weeks until my due date. It was like nesting on steroids. Sunlight streamed through the sawdust in the midst of the hottest summer in thirty years. We took out every wall on the main level, merging four rooms into one big room. If something could go wrong, it did. To save money, we did all the painting ourselves.

I covered room by room with pregnancy-safe paint. I've done lots of light remodeling, but carrying an extra eighty pounds of baby weight made it slow going. I was swollen, tired, and stressed but determined to finish.

When I painted the nursery, I hit a turning point. It was the room where I had grown up. Now my daughter would have it. If only my mom could see.

Days before my due date, only the tiny downstairs bathroom was left. I squeezed in and painted every wall but the one behind the toilet. Twisting and reaching, I coaxed the paint imperfectly into place and then realized I was stuck. My belly couldn't fit into the cramped space. I backed out, finally ready to bring our baby home.

Now we want another. That means we have to remodel the basement.

## "I CAN SEE!"

*There's something in my eye. When I rub it, it pops open. Open? What's an open eye? Blink. Now my other eye works too. Yahoo! I didn't know about this. I can see. I can see! Well, I can sort of see. When it's bright, I can make out some light through your tummy. Whoa. What was that? Flying by my eye. An arm . . . with a hand. That's my thumb. Don't mind if I give it a try. This thumb is great, but I've had it before. Now that I see it, I can come back for more.*

## BABY NOTES

Have you been nesting at all during your pregnancy? If so, what has that looked like for you?

..........................................................................

..........................................................................

..........................................................................

..........................................................................

..........................................................................

..........................................................................

..........................................................................

..........................................................................

# week TWENTY-SIX

Let's talk about glucose-tolerance tests and gestational diabetes

# week TWENTY-SIX

## I'm This Big: I'm thirteen inches long, and I weigh two pounds.

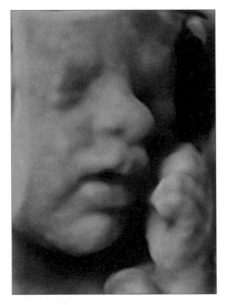

www.tyndal.es/twwyweek26

This little boy has such a sweet face. With his mouth open, he looks as if he's about to stick his little fist in it. All babies have a sucking reflex, but with some it's just ferocious. Toes, forearms, fists—whatever flies by, babies will suck into their mouths like a little vacuum. It's more common for babies to suck the sides of their hands or knuckles than their thumbs at this stage. In fact, delivery-room nurses report that some babies are born with little red marks on their hands and arms from where they were sucking. When they're born, they're usually ready to chow down.

# Development

By week twenty-six, my vocal cords are completely developed. My face is starting to look like how I will look when I'm born. I'm still very lean, but my skin is getting thicker. My nostrils are open. My eyebrows are present. I can also learn and remember.

# Rx for Health

When you're between twenty-six and twenty-eight weeks of gestation, your health-care provider will perform a glucose-tolerance test to check for diabetes. Some women may have had this test performed earlier in pregnancy depending on risk factors. Gestational diabetes affects a growing baby by causing such complications as macrosomia (large babies). If you develop diabetes during pregnancy, your provider will monitor you more closely.

**NUTRITIONAL NUGGET**
Often, gestational diabetes can be managed with proper diet and exercise. Discipline in each of these areas can keep blood-sugar levels within an acceptable range.

If you're diagnosed with gestational diabetes, you should be referred to a dietitian for advice. Controlling the amount of carbohydrates in your diet is key. That allows your body to produce the right amount of insulin. You'll need to cut back on sugar as well.

Regular exercise also helps lower blood glucose levels and makes insulin work more efficiently. Glucose levels rise after a meal, so taking a brisk walk about an hour after eating will help bring levels back down into your target range.

## MOMMY MOMENTS

### Look-Alikes

Be prepared. Everyone will take one look at your newborn and proclaim that he or she has Grandpa's ears, Great-Aunt Mary's fingers, or Mommy's eyes. Look hard enough, and baby's got a visible piece of DNA from everyone in the family. At least that's what they think.

*I was amazed at how much my second daughter looked like her sister. It was a déjà-vu experience.* —SARA LISSAUER

*Ryan looked like my husband, Mark, and Sadie looked like me. Although now, people say that Sadie is starting to look more like her father.* —JACQUE WILSON

*At birth Hannah looked exactly like my baby pictures. Chloe looked just like me, too, but with lighter hair and blue eyes.* —ELLEN BRETH

*It was hard for my husband and me to tell whom Carmen looked like after she was born. My family swore she was a mirror image of me when I was a baby, and Bryan's family said she looked like him. I could tell immediately, however, that she had Bryan's ears.* —TRICIA CAMBRON

# PRENATAL POSTCARD

## In the Family Way by Brandi Bruns

When I was pregnant with my first child, there was no doubt we would have a 3-D sonogram. We so wanted to see our baby's sweet face. On the big day, the small room was full of family. Others were online, watching the ultrasound unfold. Little Ava was quick to show she was my daughter. A few minutes into the sonogram, something amazing happened. Ava looked at the monitor and gave us her best Elvis Presley sneer. My mom and dad started laughing and said, "Oh my goodness, did she just sneer?" It took them back thirty-three years to the day of my birth.

My dad wasn't in the delivery room with my mom when I made my grand entrance. When the doctors handed me to my dad for the first time, I took one look at him and sneered. My dad thought this was funny because he is very proud of his Elvis sneer, which is a mirror image of mine. Ava has yet to show us her sneer again. But we know she can do it. Like father like daughter like granddaughter.

# "WHO DO I LOOK LIKE?"

*Who do I look like, Mom? Your side or Dad's? Do I have eyes like Uncle Bry's? Or a nose like Pa Wickersham blows? Great-Grandma thinks I'll be just like she. Short with white hair. Will that be me? Will I have teeth like Grandpa Harry? They're gone. That's scary! If I'm pretty like Lily, that will be great, or blond like my cousins Jesse, Sammy, and Jake. I could get dukes tough as Luke's, a smile big as Sadie's. Or maybe . . . When I come out, you'll see. I already look just like . . . well, me!*

## BABY NOTES

Whom in your family do you hope baby will be like and why? Whom does Dad hope baby will be like and why?

....................................................................

....................................................................

....................................................................

....................................................................

....................................................................

....................................................................

....................................................................

....................................................................

....................................................................

156

# week
# TWENTY-SEVEN

Birth plans are helpful,
but stay flexible

# week TWENTY-SEVEN

**I'M THIS BIG:** I'm fourteen inches long, and I weigh just over two pounds.

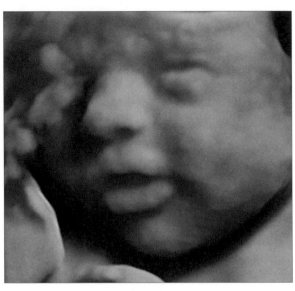

www.tyndal.es/twwyweek27

Doesn't this baby look a little mischievous? As if he's about to laugh? That slight smile speaks volumes. What thought just flashed through this wee one's head? Just before this image was captured, he was sucking and swallowing amniotic fluid. Maybe Mom had something he liked for lunch. Baby's eyes are wide open. The blur over his right eye is the placenta.

# DEVELOPMENT

By week twenty-seven, I might start to recognize different voices. My blinking reflex is also starting to develop. I can smell, and I can see some things around me.

# RX FOR HEALTH

Birth plans are a popular trend in labor and delivery. When considering drafting a birth plan, keep the ultimate goal in mind: a happy, healthy mom and baby. It's important to communicate your desires to your health-care providers, nurses, and staff, but use your plan as a guide, not as an absolute. If something doesn't go according to plan, your experience will be less fraught with disappointment if you enter the process open-minded. Birth plans cover such topics as people you want in the birthing room with you, pain management, and newborn care.

**NUTRITIONAL NUGGET**
Research shows that fish is one of the best things . . . and worst things . . . you can eat during pregnancy. As mentioned in week twenty-four, because of high mercury levels that could cause harm to the baby, the FDA advises against eating shark, swordfish, king mackerel, and tilefish during pregnancy. For the same reason, some experts also tell you to eat no more than six ounces of albacore tuna per week.[1]

On the other hand, the FDA encourages pregnant women to eat as much as twelve ounces per week of shrimp, salmon, pollock, and shellfish.[2] Some studies show that salmon reduces the risk of premature birth.[3]

## Mommy Moments
### Here's the Plan

Whether it's just a mental note or a strategically organized flow-chart, most of us make some kind of birth plan. From natural births to water births, from hospital births to home births, from planned inductions to scheduled C-sections, you have an idea what your baby's arrival will look like. Sometimes those plans work like a well-oiled, baby-birthin' machine. But sometimes surprises give way to plan B . . . or C.

*With JP, I wanted to have a natural birth, but I decided during labor that I wanted an epidural. I was happy with that experience and made a plan to opt for the epidural during my second pregnancy. However, Emily came early and fast. There was no time for an epidural. To be honest, I was so glad I didn't need it. A natural birth was the best experience ever.* —Rebecca Koeneke

*We put together a birth plan and delivered it to the hospital weeks before delivery. Early in my labor, I was asked if I wanted an epidural. My wonderful coach (aka husband) replied, "We are doing this naturally." To which a nurse said, "This baby is coming out. How much more natural do you want to get?" We ended up having a C-section. Our baby was healthy. I was healthy. It went right, just not according to our birth plan.* —Vickie Hedgepeth

*My birth plan was, "Do what is necessary to have a healthy birth." It's good I wasn't too set on a plan, because I ended up having a C-section.* —Tricia Davenport

# PRENATAL POSTCARD

## Home Birth by Janelle Stoltzfus

I was the youngest of eight. My parents were raised Amish but left that way of life before I was born. My husband was part of the Amish culture until he was seventeen. Our hearts were still steeped in the rich heritage, and we carried on many of the traditions. Many Amish women choose to give birth at home, with skilled midwives by their sides.

I remember fondly walking into my sister's bedroom the afternoon after she delivered her second daughter. I was thirteen. Peace and stillness and warmth and love engulfed the room like a warm blanket. It made a lasting impact on my impressionable self. I wanted to give birth to my babies in my own way, in my own space. So my husband and I embarked on what would be some of the greatest moments of my life on earth, laboring and delivering at home.

For our second-born, the adventure took on a deeper respect! He was born before the midwife arrived! To our shock, the contractions increased with great fervor. I stepped into the temporary birthing pool set up in our bedroom. Before I could sink down into its welcoming warmth, the baby's head appeared! I cried out to my husband. He reached down and lifted our son onto my chest. I cried and laughed while he looked around, yawning and wiggling. As he let out his first cries, our midwife ran up our old farmhouse steps!

I'm grateful for the choice we have to birth our babies at home. To pick fresh flowers and place them about, to light candles, to walk and lie down, to do whatever we feel our bodies need to do to complete this great duty. Of course, life doesn't come without searing pain. But to fully experience the hemming in of motherhood is a gift that I will always hold dear.

# TUMMY TALKIN'

*I like it when you put your hand on your tummy. It means you're thinking about me. About us. Maybe about when we'll finally meet. I already know you so well, Mom. I know what you like to eat and when. I sense when you're sad or happy or tired. I hang on every word you say . . . at least for now, anyway. And I can feel your love when you put your hand on your tummy and rub.*

## BABY NOTES

Do you have a birth plan? Jot down a few ideas for your birth plan here.

..................................................................................

..................................................................................

..................................................................................

..................................................................................

..................................................................................

..................................................................................

..................................................................................

..................................................................................

..................................................................................

..................................................................................

162

# week
# TWENTY-EIGHT

Your baby spends approximately 90 percent
of his or her time sleeping

# week TWENTY-EIGHT

**I'M THIS BIG:** I'm fourteen and a half inches long, and I weigh two and a quarter pounds.

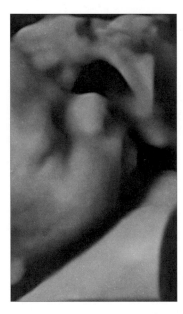

www.tyndal.es/twwyweek28

Do babies have mood swings? This little guy changed expressions faster than a cartoon character. He was wide awake and entertained his parents throughout the entire hour that they were peeking at him. Finally toward the end of the sonogram, he settled down and gave us this tender moment. He is lying on his back with his legs folded above his head. He grabbed his leg and pulled his toes to his eye for a closer look.

# Development

At twenty-eight weeks, my brain power is increasing. My hair might be getting longer too. My lungs are maturing. I have eyelashes. My eyes can produce tears. Your body is transferring many of its immunities to mine. I spend approximately 90 percent of my time sleeping.

# Rx for Health

Some studies indicate that babies consistently respond to sound stimulation starting between twenty-five and twenty-nine weeks. According to the research, what your baby hears in utero may affect speech development later. Baby may perceive rhythms and inflections from outside the womb and encode them in his or her long-term memory.

**NUTRITIONAL NUGGET**
High-calcium foods like yogurt and milk may help control fluid retention and decrease your risk of developing preeclampsia. Calcium helps form baby's connective tissue and facilitates the critical absorption of iron. It also helps with the formation of developing bones and aids in the healing process. Other natural sources of calcium include dairy, cereal, salmon, tofu, and dark-green, leafy vegetables like kale or spinach.

Babies respond differently to various types of music. If soft music is played, baby usually relaxes. Play loud music, and baby usually kicks, sometimes violently. Sounds and voices from outside the womb have to pass through air and fluid. Higher frequencies are usually filtered out. Bass or low notes in music seem to have more of an impact.

# Mommy Moments
## Music to Your Ears

From classical music to rap, babies are listening to what you are. Many mothers report that one surefire way to get their babies rockin' is to crank up the volume. Lots of moms also say slow music settles their babies down.

*My baby always kicked in the car when I played music loud. She especially liked rap and hip-hop. When her daddy talked to her, she always moved.* —Roberta Simpson

*My little one liked dance mixes on the radio and always kicked vigorously when she would hear recordings of music with my voice on it. She also kicked when her two-year-old brother, Noah, was near. I think she recognized his voice, and it made her more active.* —T. J. Kuhn

*I played Jim Brickman CDs a lot. They calmed me, and I could feel my son slow down as if they were calming him, too.* —Chris Barcus

*When I was pregnant with my son, Carlos Andres, I played those baby Mozart style CDs. I'd place the headphones on my tummy. He loves music now, including classical!* —Monica Cavazos-Rosas

# Prenatal Postcard

## "I Can Only Imagine" by Heidi Wickersham

It was an untraditional moment in a fairly traditional wedding. Instead of "The Wedding March," I walked down the aisle to the song "I Can Only Imagine." The lyrics speak of heaven. I thought of my mom who passed away eight years before. That spiritual moment when I was joined with my husband was so rich in meaning for all of us.

Four and a half years later, my husband, Matthew, was again by my side, along with my doctor and nurses.

"You are so close; keep pushing," the doctor said.

After fifty minutes of pushing, the pain was excruciating. I looked at the doctor and said, "I don't think I can keep doing this."

Just then, the first notes of "I Can Only Imagine" drifted over my iPod. It was a like a secret message of reassurance from God directly to me. "Please just turn up the music," I said. Immediately I was reenergized. As I continued to push, my doctor, nurse, and Matthew were all singing along to the song. It was one of the most touching moments of my life. Minutes later, our baby came into this world to the song "Come Thou Fount of Every Blessing." The right music at the perfect moment was a gift that helped push me past the pain to the sweet reward of our precious son.

# A SONG

*Sing me a song. Bing. Bang. Bong. Some songs make me go to sleep. Others make me kick my feet . . . to the beat. When we all go to church, and I hear the choir sing, I move to the groove. Ping. Pong. Ping. Bing. Bang. Bong. Get your groove on. Ping. Pong. Ping. Mommy, let's sing.*

## BABY NOTES

What songs do you sing to your baby? What's on your playlist for this pregnancy?

..........................................................................................

..........................................................................................

..........................................................................................

..........................................................................................

..........................................................................................

..........................................................................................

..........................................................................................

..........................................................................................

..........................................................................................

..........................................................................................

# week TWENTY-NINE

Don't stress too much over weight gain!

# week TWENTY-NINE

## I'M THIS BIG: I'm almost fifteen inches long, and I weigh 2.7 pounds.

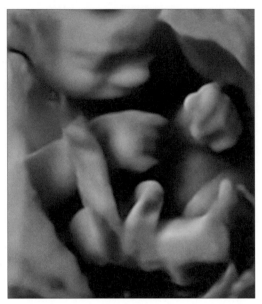

www.tyndal.es/twwyweek29

Baby is almost too big to fit all the arms and legs in one shot. This is an exception. This little one is assuming the classic fetal position. This image is a beautiful representation of what babies experience in their womb environment. The umbilical cord is a thick swirl that gently encircles the arms and body.

# Development

During the next few months, I will more than double my weight. The amniotic fluid in my sac is increasing. My pupils respond to changes in light. I start to shed some of the soft hair (lanugo) that was growing all over my body. It may be possible for someone to put an ear to your tummy and hear my heartbeat thumping from the outside.

# Rx for Health

Weight gain is expected during pregnancy. Studies support the view that too little or too much weight gain can affect a baby. It's recommended that an average woman gain between twenty-five and thirty-five pounds during pregnancy. If a woman is underweight when she becomes pregnant, that number changes to twenty-eight to forty pounds, and if a woman is overweight, fifteen to twenty-five pounds. Significantly restricting calories during your pregnancy is never recommended.

**NUTRITIONAL NUGGET**
Pregnancy is hard on your body. Beginning in your second trimester, you need an additional 340 calories a day. In your third trimester, you can eat up to 452 additional calories a day. Try to eat nutritionally dense foods when increasing your calories.[1]

# Mommy Moments
## The Weighting Game

It's the first thing your health-care provider makes you do. Step on the scale. The number staring back at you measures more than your normal weight. It's an important indicator of how your pregnancy and baby are progressing. Most moms-to-be seem to remember almost every pound and how it got there.

*It was so awesome to have an excuse to eat whenever and whatever I wanted. I used that "eating for two" thing big time!* —Kathy Haivala

*During my first pregnancy, I gained about sixty-five pounds! I broke my ankle at five months and was on bed rest by seven months due to high blood pressure. Then I developed gestational diabetes. During my second pregnancy, I gained about fifty pounds. It was a textbook pregnancy, and I liked to eat!* —Ellen Breth

*I didn't keep track of my weight that closely. I figured I was eating healthy, and there wasn't much I would do differently, so why worry? I think I gained around thirty to thirty-five pounds.* —Jacque Wilson

*When I was pregnant with my daughter, I had borderline gestational diabetes. I was so paranoid that something would happen to the baby that I never ate sugar and always combined proteins with carbs. I lost my baby weight, and more, quickly. With my second child, I didn't have the diabetes so I ate more. And it was more difficult to lose the baby weight!* —Lynne Carols

# Prenatal Postcard

## Loving My Baby Body by Samantha Krieger

"What can I get for you?" asked the spunky starbucks barista.

"Tall decaf white mocha, please," I said.

"So, is this your first?" she asked, staring at my belly.

"No, actually this is my fourth." I smiled.

"You don't look like you're on your fourth child! How old are you?"

"I know it's crazy. I'm thirty."

She gasped. "I thought you were in your twenties. Girl, you look so good—too cute!"

I laughed to myself on the way out because this lady had no idea how her words had uplifted me.

Several months before, my husband and I found out we were expecting again. This news was a complete shock—our third child was only three months old!

I had no time to get the baby weight off and had to buy larger-sized pregnancy clothes. I started developing varicose veins down my left leg that were purple and blue, and some were slightly bulging. Naturally I wanted to hide my leg and wear jeans even in the one-hundred-degree Texas heat. But I also wanted to find humor and acceptance in these bizarre changes in my body. I could either be upset by the changes or embrace them. After all, this pregnancy was God's gift to our family.

God wanted me to be thankful. One day I'd miss having a baby bump and feeling a jab or a roll inside my belly. I'd miss the maternity clothes, baby showers, and the whole labor-and-delivery experience.

When I accepted my body as it was, I found joy in the journey of the unexpected. I wore skirts and shorts without shame. I chose to dwell on encouraging words from people like the starbucks barista and, most of all, God's truth.

I'm six weeks away from delivering our son. I can't wait to kiss his soft skin and hold him in my arms. I'm praying these varicose veins will disappear, but if they don't or if a few remain, it won't be the end of the world!

# ICE CREAM

*You know what I like, Mom? Ice cream. Isn't it good? Chocolate and caramel.*
*Vanilla with strawberries. I wish I could have some every day. Times three. That would*
*be yummy. And cookies. Cookies are great. With more ice cream and cake. I know*
*you're trying not to gain too much weight. To take good care of me . . . and you. But*
*couldn't we have some dessert? 'Cause when I come out, I won't get it for months!*

## BABY NOTES

How much baby weight have you put on? How are you feeling about
your baby body right now?

........................................................................................

........................................................................................

........................................................................................

........................................................................................

........................................................................................

........................................................................................

........................................................................................

........................................................................................

........................................................................................

# week
# THIRTY

Be aware of what is going on
with your baby

# week THIRTY

**I'M THIS BIG:** I'm fifteen and one-third inches long, and I weigh about three pounds.

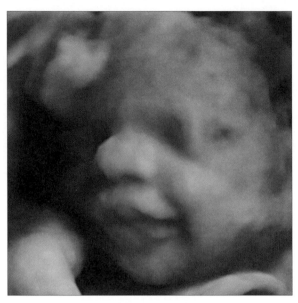

www.tyndal.es/twwyweek30

Who says babies don't smile until at least three weeks after they're born? No one knows what prompts it, but sonographers see babies smile before they're born all the time, sometimes as early as twenty-five weeks. This chubby-cheeked baby is only a few months from birth, and look at that smile. It's magical! Sometimes it's just a quick smirk or grin, and sometimes sonographers capture a full-blown smile. Don't attribute this to gas pains. Remember, there's no air in that amniotic fluid. By the way, that "smudge" over baby's eyes is actually the placenta.

# Development

By week thirty, a doctor might be able to tell what position I'm in by feeling your stomach. My brain is growing in size. I might have a good head of hair. My skin is still slightly wrinkled. There's not much room in your uterus. I kick you when I'm in an uncomfortable position. If my head is down, I may kick hard into your ribs. If I'm in a breech position, I may kick your bladder.

# Rx for Health

Always be aware of what is going on with your baby, especially when it comes to movement. If you're concerned because of a decrease in your baby's activity, you may want to start kick counts. It's best to lie on your left side; this increases blood flow to the baby. If you don't have gestational diabetes, drink a glass of juice. This may direct glucose to the baby and cause some stimulation. Concentrate only on your baby and start counting how many times you feel movement, big or small. If you don't feel at least ten movements in two hours, you should call your health-care provider for advice.

**NUTRITIONAL NUGGET**
Baby needs cholesterol right now to form his or her nervous system, so if you have your blood tested for cholesterol and triglycerides during pregnancy, don't be alarmed if your levels are elevated. They normally increase during pregnancy, especially during the third trimester. Your levels will probably stay elevated if you breastfeed. If you're especially concerned, ask your doctor or test your levels again after you've weaned your baby.

Baby may be swallowing up to an ounce of amniotic fluid a day. This helps the digestive system prepare for life outside the womb. It also helps develop baby's sucking reflex, which is necessary for nursing or drinking from a bottle.

## Mommy Moments

### Out of the Mouths of Babes

At this stage of the game, most women are feeling a little large and in charge. You know it, and you probably don't want to hear about weight gain from anyone else. But sometimes the little people in your life just can't help but wonder!

*I taught swimming lessons until I was thirty-six weeks pregnant. When I was well into my third trimester, one of my students pointed to my belly and asked what was in there. I told him a baby. He then promptly swam around behind me and pointed to my rear end and asked me what was in there!*
—Rebecca Miljavac

*I told my three-year-old niece that there was a baby in my tummy while showing her my bare stomach. She looked at me, mortified, and asked, "You ate her?" I thought I was going to laugh myself into labor!*
—Rebecca Blair Pettegrew

*My three-year-old asked if the doctor was going to take all my teeth out . . . so I wouldn't hurt the baby on its way out.* —Yvonne Baltezor

*When I was pregnant with my third, my seven-year-old asked me one day out of the blue, "How did the baby get in your belly?" As I stared at him blankly, processing what he was asking me, he followed it up with, "Did you pray to God?" To which I gladly responded, "Yeah! Something like that."*
—Janet Aughinbaugh

# PRENATAL POSTCARD

## Twice the Fun by Kara Broeker

An early sonogram revealed that we had not one but two babies on the way. As they grew, I could feel two sets of feet, elbows, and hands constantly turning and prodding. We loved the biweekly sonograms.

It didn't take long to discover that our girls were very different. We called Berkley "the bruiser." She moved and changed directions each week. Kinley stayed in virtually the same position until they were born at thirty-six weeks. Wouldn't you know that Berkley is now our little busy bee? A very free spirit, she never stands still, while Kinley is quiet and observant.

The babies slept together in the beginning. In almost all of their first baby pictures, they are touching in some way. They even sucked on each other's hands. Berkley and Kinley are still complete opposites in looks and personality, yet they're inseparable. They play together, want to do everything at the same time, and will wait for the other one to arrive before they do something fun. The bond they have is amazing. It was born long before they were.

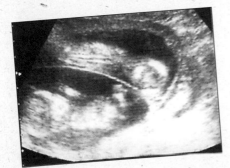

Baby girls at sixteen weeks gestation

Berkley and Kinley at three weeks old

# "I'M SQUISHED"

*I used to have more room than this. I remember doing double flips. Now I'm squished.*
*I try to stretch. I try to play. Nope. I can't. Things are in the way. I think things like*
*your ribs. Could you move them a little bit? They are poking me. Can't you see?*
*I need more space. Maybe I should think about moving out of this place.*

## BABY NOTES

Now is a great time for you (or Dad) to start reading to your baby.
Just pick a few books and read them regularly. You might ask friends
to recommend popular children's books; then go ahead and start
building up baby's library! List a few ideas here.

..............................................................................................

..............................................................................................

..............................................................................................

..............................................................................................

..............................................................................................

..............................................................................................

..............................................................................................

..............................................................................................

# week THIRTY-ONE

Reducing your stress level
helps you and baby

# week THIRTY-ONE

**I'M THIS BIG:** I'm fifteen and three-quarters inches long, and I weigh three and one-quarter pounds.

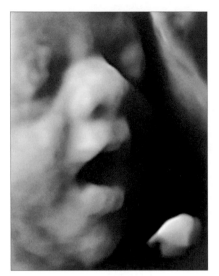

www.tyndal.es/twwyweek31

It makes us sleepy just to watch this baby yawn. But studies show that fatigue or boredom probably isn't the cause of this little one's big yawn. There is obviously no air in the womb, so the yawn doesn't deliver oxygen the way it does when we yawn. Research indicates that babies yawn the most before twenty-eight weeks. Some scientists suspect the action in some way helps the brain mature.[1]

## DEVELOPMENT

By week thirty-one, I can focus on things several inches in front of my face. And I'm getting smarter. I'm starting to control my own body temperature. My motor skills are becoming more refined.

# Rx for Health

Start getting ready for labor now. Exercise will probably make it easier. A good workout also prevents leg cramps and constipation. With medical approval, prenatal yoga, walking, swimming, and stationary cycling are great exercise options during pregnancy. Also try squats, pelvic tilts, and Kegel exercises to prepare for labor.

Because pregnancy so drastically changes your body, here are a few things to beware of while exercising:

1. Breathlessness—Your respiratory rate increases when you're pregnant to ensure that baby is getting enough oxygen. If you're overdoing it, you can easily become breathless. Slow your pace until your breathing returns to normal.

2. Loss of balance—As baby grows, your center of gravity changes. The hormone relaxin has already loosened your joints and ligaments, so you may lose your balance more easily and become more susceptible to sprains and strains. So take it easy.

3. Overheating—Your core body temperature is already higher than normal, so if you're exercising in the heat, be careful. Getting really hot can hurt the baby. Drink plenty of fluids and don't overdo it.

4. Light-headedness—Your metabolism kicks into a higher gear during pregnancy, and exercise speeds it up even more. That means you could become light-headed, often because your blood sugar drops too low. If you become light-headed, sit down, drink something, and have a healthy snack.

**NUTRITIONAL NUGGET**
Staying well hydrated during your pregnancy is important for the production of amniotic fluid as well as to decrease uterine contractions. If you become dehydrated, your uterus may be more likely to contract. The amount of fluid intake needed during pregnancy may vary depending on the situation. For example, if you have excessive vomiting or diarrhea or even sweating on a hot day, you'll require more fluids. If you feel as if you've become dehydrated for whatever reason, it's best to contact your healthcare provider to see if you may need intravenous (IV) hydration.

# MOMMY MOMENTS
## Then and Now

The pregnancy experience has definitely changed in the past few decades. Most of our mothers never had sonograms, paid maternity leave, or for that matter, the option to intentionally give birth in a tub of warm scented water serenaded by hypnotic, pain-relieving music. Times have changed, but it sure is fun to hear about the good ole days.

*When my sister had her first baby in 1965, her husband had to sneak me up to her room under his long coat because I was too young to visit the maternity ward. I was fourteen!* —INGRID BRUNS

*In 1986, I had a C-section. They knocked me out with gas. I woke up two hours later repeatedly asking, "What did we have?"* —SANDY TREWETT

*When my first child was born fifty years ago, my husband couldn't be near the labor and delivery ward. While I was having contractions, he was having breakfast in the cafeteria. By the way, the hospital bill was twenty-five dollars.* —PATTY RIDDLE

*Fifty years ago, I had my first son in a small-town maternity home. There was no such thing as an epidural, only a localized shot to numb some of the pain. The nurses changed my son's diapers and brought me my meals and taught me to feed, burp, and bathe my baby. It was like a wonderful five-day vacation.* —IRENE HAIVALA

# PRENATAL POSTCARD

## Back in the Day by Linda Manhart

In 1979, I was pregnant for the fourth time. We already had three girls. This was our last shot at a boy. Small Illinois town. Smaller hospital. No ultrasounds. So the chance of discovering our baby's gender before delivery day was zero.

Three days before my due date, I was lying in the delivery room with no option of an epidural. I gave birth to a five-pound, four-ounce baby girl. The doctor held her up for me to see, and we admired her full head of hair. She was beautiful. He handed her to the nurse and went back to the task at hand.

That's when I heard him exclaim, "Wait a minute!" The clock on the wall ticked, and I started pushing . . . again.

Nineteen minutes later, little Beth was born.

I was floored!

The nurse found my unsuspecting husband in the waiting room. "Congratulations. You have twin girls!" she said. My husband grinned and said, "I knew we should have bought stock in Kotex."

Three days later, I had my tubes tied. Boy or no boy, we were done increasing the population of Shelby, Illinois.

Eight months later, I began to feel violently ill. My doctor told me that there were two possibilities: (1) I had a tumor, or (2) I was pregnant.

Turns out, I was four and a half months pregnant . . . and very relieved I wasn't dying. The doctor listened to the slow, steady thump-thump of the baby's heartbeat and, based on that alone, wrote "It's a boy" on my records.

For the first time, as I went into labor, my husband was allowed in the delivery room. It was an easy birth, and my husband and I celebrated together as our first boy came kicking into the world. In one breath I whispered, "Thank You, Lord, and I have no idea how to take care of a boy!"

By the way, as soon as Zachary was born, I made my husband get a vasectomy.

# A WALK

*Mom, let's go for a walk. Sometimes I'm restless just sitting around. I get a bit fussy till your feet hit the ground. And then . . . I feel better. It's the rhythmic clip-clop of your wobbly walk. It rocks me to sleep when you move your feet. Not too fast. Don't bump me and make me all jumpy. I just like a slow trot when we're taking a walk.*

## BABY NOTES

How's your stress level at this point in your pregnancy? What helps you relax?

........................................................................................

........................................................................................

........................................................................................

........................................................................................

........................................................................................

........................................................................................

........................................................................................

........................................................................................

........................................................................................

# week THIRTY-TWO

Have you signed up for
prenatal education classes?

# week THIRTY-TWO

*A happy family is but an earlier heaven.*
—George Bernard Shaw

## I'm This Big: I'm sixteen inches long, and I weigh three and a half pounds.

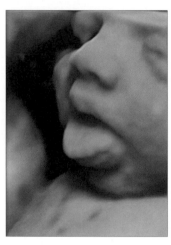

www.tyndal.es/twwyweek32

Babies build their digestive systems before birth by swallowing plenty of amniotic fluid. This baby seems pretty happy with whatever flavor just hit her taste buds. Baby is practicing sucking, swallowing, and tasting. This early eating causes baby to crave the flavors in mother's milk as soon as she is born.

# DEVELOPMENT

At thirty-two weeks, my chest and diaphragm are working together with my lungs. I have a regular pattern of sleep and activity. My knees are usually pressed into my chest. My body is filling out. If I'm a boy, my testes are descending. You can even see my toenails.

# RX FOR HEALTH

If you haven't already, sign up for prenatal education classes. Try a childbirth or breastfeeding class. Classes on general labor processes and expectations are often more beneficial than limiting yourself to a particular method. Because labor is so unpredictable, it's best to be ready for anything. Parenting classes on infant care, infant first aid and CPR, or infant massage are best taken before baby is born.

   If you are planning a hospital birth, now is the time to set up a tour. Doing a walk-through helps you visualize your labor-and-delivery process and get any final questions answered. Becoming familiar with the layout and staff will probably also make you feel more comfortable when it's actually "go time."

**NUTRITIONAL NUGGET**
If you're looking for a prenatal smoothie that packs a big nutritional punch, savor this!

1 cup orange or apple juice
1/2 cup frozen banana (potassium)
1/2 cup strawberries (vitamin C)
1/2 cup spinach (iron)
2 tablespoons whey protein (for muscles)
2 tablespoons flax, freshly ground (adds fiber for constipation)
1 tablespoon wheat germ (B vitamins)

Blend well and enjoy!

This is a perfect time to reduce your level of stress, anxiety, or discomfort while getting your partner involved in bonding with baby. Some of these techniques can help now and during labor:

- Get a massage! Whether it's a professional massage or your partner's touch, massage will enhance your comfort level.
- Massage or have your partner massage your belly and respond to your baby's increasing movement. Responding to kicks and movement are the beginnings of early communication with your baby.
- Encourage your partner to talk to baby. It will help baby recognize voices of those closest to him or her on birth day.[1]

# MOMMY MOMENTS

## A Talk with Dad

Because baby can hear during the entire third trimester, many parents spend daily time communicating with him or her. This can be especially important for daddy-baby bonding. Sometimes all that talking pays off with a look of recognition on delivery day.

*My husband read psalms and other poetry to our son. I sang and played music a lot.* —AILENE BANKS

*My husband would talk to my belly a lot. When Jesse was born, he knew his daddy's voice immediately.* —JENNIFER WICKERSHAM

*While I was pregnant with our son, Joey, there were many nights my husband would play the violin for our baby.* —NANCY YOUREE

*My husband read Curious George books to our son while I was pregnant.* —BECKY MORRELL

*My husband would rub my stomach and talk to Brandon, and Brandon would usually kick. After Brandon was born, he would turn his head to the sound of my husband's voice.* —CELESTE KIRMER

*Each time I was pregnant, my husband would kiss and talk to my belly often, telling our babies how much he loved them and all the things he hoped to do with them.* —BRANDY BRUCE

# Prenatal Postcard

## Internet Connection by Lynn Jasper

While contractions gripped me and squeezed my voice silent, my husband sat shivering in a hallway thousands of miles away. I could hear the sound of his voice encouraging me. Peter leaned into his computer.

I looked over at him in his crumpled army uniform, the same one he had worn for more than twenty-four hours, and I was thankful for the technology that allowed us to experience this moment together.

My water broke the night before at my parents' home. That's where I was staying during Peter's tour of duty in Afghanistan. My due date was still a couple of weeks away, so he wasn't expecting the urgent call so soon.

Peter was sitting in a briefing when someone passed him a two-word message. "Baby. NOW!" He rushed toward the computer in his room . . . his tasks momentarily excused.

It was our first baby. Neither of us knew quite what to expect.

For eleven hours we talked, screen to screen.

He met the nurses and doctors. And finally his daughter.

The computer captured her robust cry along with Peter's tears of joy and relief.

As doctors worked on me, my dad picked up the laptop and followed our baby to the warmer. Peter waved and talked to his new daughter.

Afghanistan time, it was nearly 6:00 a.m. Four weeks would pass before my husband could come home and hold the little girl he had grown to love through an Internet connection. We are so thankful for the technology that is bridging that distance for military families all over the world.

## "MY DAD"

*Is there someone else besides you and me, Mom? I can hear him sometimes. He sounds pretty strong. Is he bigger than me? We'll see about that. I'll show him who's boss when I drool down his back! Is he worried about me? What to do . . . what to say? Just tell him when I get there, I'll show him the way. And then he can show me some stuff too.*

## BABY NOTES

Tell baby about his or her father.

.........................................................................................................

.........................................................................................................

.........................................................................................................

.........................................................................................................

.........................................................................................................

.........................................................................................................

.........................................................................................................

.........................................................................................................

.........................................................................................................

.........................................................................................................

192

# week THIRTY-THREE

Baby is probably having his or her own dreams

# week THIRTY-THREE

**I'M THIS BIG:** I'm sixteen and a half inches long, and I weigh four pounds.

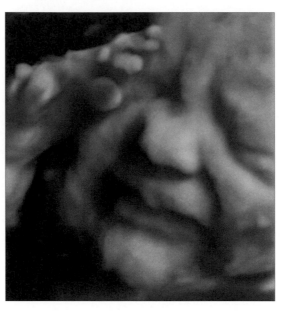

www.tyndal.es/twwyweek33

Isn't it amazing how much emotion can be emitted by a thirty-three-week-old baby? The furrowed brow and angry, wrinkled nose make this baby look flat-out frustrated. Who knows exactly what baby is thinking? Baby was sleeping just moments before, with her head tucked into Mom's uterine wall. To get a better shot, the sonographer pressed gently on the mother's abdomen. Baby's reaction was immediate annoyance. Mom may need a sign on the nursery door: "Baby sleeping. She gets angry when awakened unexpectedly."

# Development

At thirty-three weeks, I can suck and swallow, and my lungs are practicing breathing movements, which means that if I were to be born now, I might not need a feeding tube. I'm probably having my own dreams. I'm also developing more of my own personality.

# Rx for Health

If you sleep on your back during this stage of pregnancy, you'll probably feel uncomfortable and short of breath. That discomfort is designed to keep your baby safe. It's best to sleep on your left side because it will take the weight of the uterus off the large blood vessels that carry blood to and from your heart. It also allows for the most blood flow to your baby through the placenta.

**NUTRITIONAL NUGGET**
Hormonal changes combined with the extra iron in your prenatal vitamin can cause constipation—or even hemorrhoids—during pregnancy. Some natural ways to combat constipation are increasing your fluid consumption (mostly water) and gentle exercise. Also try to add more fruits, veggies, and whole grains to your diet. If that doesn't work, contact your health-care provider about a stool softener.

# MOMMY MOMENTS

## Bed Rest

It can happen when you least expect it. The order to get off your feet and into bed sounds like blissful medicine for a day, but when it drags on and on, it's difficult on a lot of levels. Here's some advice about how to make the best of bed rest from moms who have been there:

*Bed rest was one of the hardest things I had to do with Hannah's pregnancy! I had high blood pressure, gestational diabetes, possible preeclampsia, and a broken ankle! My mom was a lifesaver, but it was hard to watch others do everything for me.* —ELLEN BRETH

*I was ordered to bed rest at twenty-one weeks after I went to the doctor and was dilated to three centimeters. It was very scary. I was sure we were going to lose our twins. No one thought I would make it through the weekend. I stayed in the hospital for fifty days. I went into labor at twenty-eight weeks and had my babies! Just know that this too will pass, and you'll have a lot to show for it.* —SHANNON KAUFFMAN

*I was put on bed rest at thirty-two weeks and stayed there until I delivered. My mom and sister were my angels. They came over daily, bringing food and stuff for the baby, helped clean, and got things ready. My advice to other moms in this situation is simply to* accept help! *It's the best thing you can do to alleviate the stress of being on bed rest.* —AMANDA STRAUB

# PRENATAL POSTCARD

## "He's Got the Little, Bitty Babies . . ."
by Nicole Sedelmeier

Two months before my daughter's due date, I felt a gentle voice inside tell me that I needed to get ready. Things were going to happen sooner than expected. My husband and best friend both thought I was cleaning and nesting way too early.

A few days later, during a routine exam, the sonographer grew quiet. Medical staff ushered me to a room and put straps around my belly that connected to monitors. No one would look at me. I could see their worried faces and hear them whisper in the hall. My three-year-old son, Tristan, looked frightened. I tried to stay calm.

My daughter was measuring small. The doctor scheduled more tests, prescribed partial bed rest, and warned about a possible early induction. God told me that a week before the appointment. I just didn't know it was Him.

I went home terrified. My husband was already working two jobs. Now he would have to take on more duties at home.

As I dressed Tristan for bed, I finally broke down. I was crying into my hands when Tristan put his gentle, little fingers on my pregnant belly. Through teary eyes, I looked up at him and listened. He cupped his hands into a tiny cradle and sang. "He's got the little, bitty babies in His hands . . ." He held his hands out to me again, his only physical connection to his sister. I was astonished. Tears of thanksgiving flowed for the two blessings before me. One of those blessings stood with a look of complete calm in his tender, brown eyes. The other blessing stretched and strained for more room in my increasingly protruding belly.

Through Tristan, God gave me peace. He reminded me that my baby girl is His daughter first. He had talked me into getting ready early. He would guide my sweet Eliana into this world to live up to her name, which means "my God has answered."

# THE DREAM

*While I slept today, I had a deep thought. I think it was a dream. I dreamed I was going through a dark tunnel toward a light. It was bright. I heard the voice I always hear. Everyone cheered. But I cried. Because it wasn't the same as inside. Then it got better 'cause you held me tight. You whispered that everything would be all right. I wonder if there's anything to that light, or if it was only a dream.*

## BABY NOTES

What's still on your to-do list to accomplish before baby is born?

..................................................................................

..................................................................................

..................................................................................

..................................................................................

..................................................................................

..................................................................................

..................................................................................

..................................................................................

..................................................................................

..................................................................................

# week THIRTY-FOUR

Baby's organs are almost mature

# week THIRTY-FOUR

I'M THIS BIG: I'm seventeen inches long, and I weigh four and a half pounds.

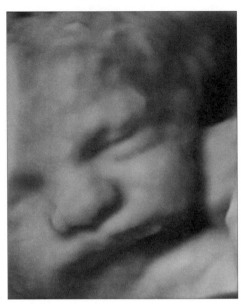

www.tyndal.es/twwyweek34

No, you're not having a close encounter with a *Star Trek* character. The wrinkles that look as if they're rippling out of this baby's head are, in fact, hair. A sonographer can typically see hair from thirty weeks on. Curly hair is denser and easier to see. If you can see thick hair in a sonogram, you can be sure baby will have a head full when he or she is born.

# Development

At thirty-four weeks, my organs are almost mature. I have thick vernix all over my body. I can blink. My skin is now smooth. My fingernails have reached my fingertips. My head may now be positioned down toward your pelvis.

# Rx for Health

At this stage of pregnancy, your health-care provider would be less likely to use medical interventions to prevent delivery if you were to go into labor. It's best to carry your baby to term, but studies show that after thirty-four weeks of gestation, most babies will do well outside the uterus but will still require a stay in the neonatal nursery. If there's a concern about preterm delivery, your health-care practitioner may suggest bed rest to prolong your pregnancy.

**NUTRITIONAL NUGGET**
In recent years, much has been said about the possible benefits of the omega-3 fatty acid DHA and its link to brain development in a baby. Some research indicates that infants born to mothers with higher blood levels of DHA have longer attention spans well into their second year of life.[1] Atlantic salmon, Pacific codfish, and tuna are some of the best food sources of DHA. Aim for six to twelve ounces of DHA-rich fish a week.

# Mommy Moments
## Tuck 'n' Roll

Nothing else feels like a baby rolling around inside you. It's hard to explain to anyone who hasn't felt it. It can be comforting, embarrassing, painful, or exhilarating. But if there's one thing most women miss about being pregnant, it's feeling their baby so snug and secure inside of them.

*My family could see and feel him move. We could see a hand or a foot from time to time. It was just amazing to see that little person in there. When he rolled, you could see his little bum. So sweet.* —Chris Barcus

*Occasionally, family and friends could see the baby move from outside. My single brother was freaked out; he thought it looked like an alien. My husband thought it was a little odd as well, but he was fascinated. My mom loved it. That is my favorite thing about pregnancy, seeing and feeling the baby move!* —Ellen Breth

*My son loves to put his hand on my tummy now and feel his sisters. Their movements are getting so strong and pronounced. He always asks me if it hurts and if it felt the same when he was inside me. My husband loves to put his hand on my stomach while I'm sleeping; he says he doesn't know how I sleep through the movement.* —Kara Broeker

# PRENATAL POSTCARD

## Forget Something? by Christina Gebhardt

If pregnancy stories were movies, mine would be on the blooper reel. It was my first time. How was I to know my contractions would go from zero to sixty like a Ferrari setting a land speed record?

Only an hour before, they were five minutes apart. Now my sister and brother-in-law were frantically helping me down the hall to my husband, who had grabbed my suitcase and bolted out the door.

I thought he would be waiting to lovingly assist me into our new Ford Ranger. Instead, as I crossed the threshold, the brake lights flashed, and I heard the squeal of rubber as I watched him careen down the road without me.

Tears of pain and disbelief streamed down my face. But he came back. And he dropped the tailgate. The tailgate! That was where he wanted me and my amniotic-leaking sac to park it on the way to the hospital. After all, the suitcase was occupying the perfectly clean passenger seat.

"Move the suitcase!" I yelled. "I am not tailgating to the hospital!"

My contractions were now two minutes apart.

My husband jerked the luggage out so fast that it burst open, spewing maternity cargo all over the wet driveway. Rattled by my yelling at him, he began to fold the clothes and return them to their rightful place.

I was beside myself. "Just cram them in there, and let's go!" I screamed. My flustered husband couldn't even speak.

That's probably why he took a wrong turn. We ended up on the wrong highway headed in the opposite direction of any kind of medical help. Between short, shallow breaths, I went ballistic.

Finally we arrived at the hospital, and because of dehydration, my labor came to a screeching halt. Thirteen painful hours later, our son was born, blissfully unaware of the wild ride we took to welcome him.

# HEAD DOWN

*I'm scooting and squirming, inching my way around. So my bum will point up, and my head will face down. It's tighter in here than you'll ever believe; not even enough room for a butterfly sneeze. Please, Mom, sit still. I'm trying to budge. Maybe this would be easier if I weren't such a pudge. I have to get busy. Can't sit here and pout. I need my head down so I can get out!*

## BABY NOTES

Have you packed your baby bag yet? Toured the hospital? What are you planning to take with you?

.................................................................................

.................................................................................

.................................................................................

.................................................................................

.................................................................................

.................................................................................

.................................................................................

.................................................................................

.................................................................................

# week THIRTY-FIVE

The last few weeks of baby's time in the womb are consumed by weight gain

# week THIRTY-FIVE

**I'M THIS BIG:** I'm seventeen and a half inches long, and I weigh five pounds.

*I kind of started sweating, which I guess is a normal thing, but then, all of a sudden, in front of all my friends, my water broke! It was like a romantic comedy.*
—JENNA BUSH HAGER

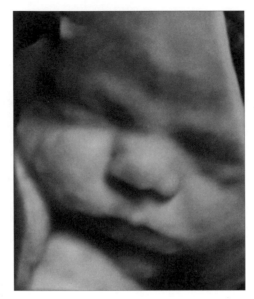

www.tyndal.es/twwyweek35

The baby's main job during the last few weeks in the womb is to gain weight. You can see this little one's face fleshing out. Those chubby cheeks are preparing for their entrance. Notice this baby's button nose.

# DEVELOPMENT

At thirty-five weeks, my skin is pink because of fat deposits underneath it. The fat will help me stay warm after I'm born. During the next few weeks, I will gain between five and twelve ounces a week. If your finger were nearby, I'm strong enough now to grasp it firmly in my hand. My limbs are usually flexed because of lack of space.

# Rx for Health

During the last few weeks of pregnancy, your body produces more of the hormone relaxin. It allows the pelvis to widen in preparation for delivery. This process may result in increased pelvic pressure and pain in your hip joints and pubic bone. To relieve pressure and discomfort, try using baby belts and pillows while sitting or lying down. Sometime between thirty-five and thirty-seven weeks, your provider will perform a test looking for a bacteria called group B streptococcus. This test is done rectovaginally using a cotton swab. If you are a carrier of this common bacteria, you will receive antibiotics in labor to decrease the risk that your baby will be exposed.

**NUTRITIONAL NUGGET**
Third-trimester nutrition is important. It will give you energy for labor and help with breast-milk production. So even if you don't feel like it, eat small, frequent meals packed with calcium, protein, and iron. You can find some delicious and healthy recipe suggestions online, such as Sunflower Seed and Caramelized Onion Frittata (see notes section for full recipe!).[1]

For specific nutrition guidelines to meet your pregnancy needs, go to www.choosemyplate.gov. This website will tailor a personalized menu plan based on information you enter into the SuperTracker program.

# MOMMY MOMENTS

## Coming Undone

This is the hard part. Whether you're ready or not, baby launch is T minus five weeks and counting. Growing tired? Getting excited? Nervous? Probably a little of each.

*With my first pregnancy, I had gestational diabetes. By the end, I was tired of doctor's appointments, a special diet, and urine collection for analysis. Physically I was uncomfortable. With my second pregnancy, I didn't have time to think about it because I was busy chasing a two-year-old around!* —ELLEN BRETH

*I was so ready to see my babies and hold them. My husband and I got the nursery ready and had lots of showers held for us.* —JACQUE WILSON

*By the end of my first pregnancy, I felt so uncomfortable that my husband, Mike, had to sleep on the couch because of all the pillows I needed just to try to sleep and to get comfortable!* —NISHA LOWE

*As I neared the end of my pregnancy, I was ready to stop being pregnant! I would look longingly at clothes in the store windows at the mall and feel like I would never get to wear something normal again.* —TRICIA CAMBRON

# PRENATAL POSTCARD

## Confessions of a Working Pregnant Woman by April Hawley

As a busy professional pregnant for the first time, I assumed I could pull off twelve- to fourteen-hour working days and glide through growing another human being without it changing anything other than the physical appearance of my bump. I was wrong! That just wasn't my experience.

I couldn't believe how exhausted I was! During my first and third trimesters, I would take a nap in my office at work every day. Every single day. I would close my office door and lock it and then lie down on the hard floor with my coat crumpled up under my head and sleep. Mind you, my office was on the executive floor. People would be knocking on the door, and I would be lying down trying to catch a few winks. It was either that or have my colleagues find me slumped over my keyboard drooling and dreaming!

I don't think I was fooling anyone, though. After "naptime" my hair was usually disheveled, and my makeup was worn off. My hips would be sore from lying on the floor on my side, especially during the third trimester. I was trying to figure out how I could discreetly bring in extra pillows to lie on, all the while passing them off as decorative throw pillows on the chairs around my conference table!

# BIG ENOUGH

*When will I be big enough to come out there and play? By my calculations, it should be any day. When will I grow tall enough to pick out what I eat? Have a toy with a horn that goes beep, beep? Cross the street? Go to my friend's house to sleep? Not yet, you say? Well, okay. How about sleep with no night-light or ride a big bike? Buy a car? Drive really far? Swim at the pool? Go to school? Ride the bus? Have a date? What's the fuss? I'll have to wait! But Mom, I'm growing quickly. I'm really pretty strong. Getting big enough for some stuff takes way too long.*

## BABY NOTES

Write a wish for your baby today. (Or have Dad write a wish if you want!)

........................................................................

........................................................................

........................................................................

........................................................................

........................................................................

........................................................................

........................................................................

........................................................................

........................................................................

210

# week THIRTY-SIX

Choosing a name for your baby is an important (and fun!) decision

# week THIRTY-SIX

**I'M THIS BIG:** I'm eighteen inches long, and I weigh five and a half pounds.

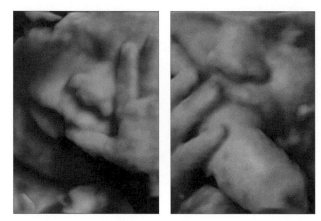

www.tyndal.es/twwyweek36

This little guy had his hands all over his face. Within seconds he had his fingers up his nose and his entire fist in his mouth. He then raised his hand over his face in a "stop" motion, suggesting he had had just about enough of our intrusion. Baby is probably moving a little less these days because of reduced amniotic fluid and limited real estate.

A mother is the truest friend we have, when trials heavy and sudden, fall upon us; when adversity takes the place of prosperity; when friends who rejoice with us in our sunshine desert us; when trouble thickens around us, still will she cling to us, and endeavor by her kind precepts and counsels to dissipate the clouds of darkness, and cause peace to return to our hearts.
—WASHINGTON IRVING

# Development

By week thirty-six, I'm now gaining nearly one ounce a day. It's tight in here. I can distinguish differences in the sounds I hear outside the womb, including different voices.

# Rx for Health

At this time your body may increase its production of the hormone oxytocin. This hormone is responsible for uterine contractions and the release of mother's milk. You may start to notice more contractions, especially in the middle of the night. Oxytocin is released in greater amounts at night, which is why so many babies are born in the middle of the night!

**NUTRITIONAL NUGGET**
As your body prepares for labor and delivery, you need more of two nutrients: magnesium and zinc. Magnesium is for building healthy bones and tissues. It also supports the immune system. During pregnancy, you need 350 mg of magnesium per day.[1] Good sources of magnesium include low-fat milk; peanuts; bananas; wheat germ; dark-green, leafy vegetables; and oysters. Zinc can help prevent preterm delivery and promotes endurance and healing. The recommended daily intake of zinc for pregnant and lactating women is 11–12 mg per day.[2] You can find zinc in wheat bran, eggs, nuts, onions, shellfish, sunflower seeds, wheat germ, whole wheat, lean meat, turkey, dried beans, and peas.

## MOMMY MOMENTS

### The Name Game

It's one of those decisions forever etched in stone. You look at it from every angle. Will this name work for my child as an adult? Does it speak of greatness or cuteness? Does it rhyme with anything gross? Does it flow with the middle name and last name . . . because you know someday you'll pull out your big-mama voice and string all three of them together.

> *With the first baby, we knew we were having a girl, and we really liked the name Jaide. Then we found the name Jaiden, which means "God has heard" in Hebrew. We had tried for a while to get pregnant with her, and when we found the name, we knew God had heard our prayers, so it was fitting.*
> —CHRISTIANE BRANSTROM

> *My husband and I knew early on that we wanted our son to be named Ryan. It means "little king." A few years later, when we were looking for a name for our daughter, we discovered that Sadie's name meant "princess." It just fit.*
> —JACQUE WILSON

> *My husband picked Dylan's first name, but his middle name came from a late night of watching the Dick Van Dyke Show. The Petries had named their son Richard "Rosebud." Ritchie was horrified when his friends found out, but his parents explained that it was an acronym. I loved this, and we came up with "Jarrec" for Dylan's middle name, made from the names of special people in our lives.* —KARLA SHOTTS

# PRENATAL POSTCARD

## What's in a Name? by Mary Pulley

I felt that choosing a name for our baby was one of the most important decisions we'd make in this journey. It sticks with the kid for life, after all! Once we found out we were having a boy, it was time to choose a name. Thoughts ran through my mind: This little baby has already come to mean so much to me, and now it's time for him to have his own identity. So what do we call him? I've lived my whole life with such a simple and common name. Do I give him a biblical name with a strong meaning indicating his purpose or destiny? What about a family name to honor a relative I deeply respect? Maybe I could go all Hollywood and give him a crazy name like Electric Cider or something!

When it came down to it, I knew I wanted a name that would just roll off the tongue. And we had a name that fulfilled everything we wanted. In all honesty, this little boy's name was chosen long ago, back when I was a teenager. My husband and I were high school sweethearts and have been together since the ages of fifteen and sixteen. Way back then, when the thought of marriage and family was a distant idea, we had a conversation about what our child's name would be.

We had tossed around names and said that if we had a daughter, we'd name her Maranda. It's a mix of our names, Mary and Randall. When it came to a son, we decided on Landen. It has the same letters as my husband's name (except for the e) and sounds similar to his. But most important, we both loved the way it sounded.

We just needed to choose baby Landen's middle name. We wanted to honor my husband's father, James, which is also a biblical name.

So there you have it! Landen James.

# "YOUR VOICE"

*I hear you, Mom. I know who you are. I know how you feel by the sound of
your voice. I listen. You sing. You laugh. Yell at the dog. Talk to friends. I like
it best when you talk to me. Or read to me. Our own conversations are the
richest. When I get there, I'll find you. I'll know you by your voice.*

## BABY NOTES

What baby names are you considering and why? Do you call baby
by a nickname now?

..............................................................................................

..............................................................................................

..............................................................................................

..............................................................................................

..............................................................................................

..............................................................................................

..............................................................................................

..............................................................................................

..............................................................................................

..............................................................................................

216

# week THIRTY-SEVEN

Baby may be engaging in the pelvis (dropping) about now

# week THIRTY-SEVEN

## I'M THIS BIG: I'm nineteen inches long, and I weigh six pounds.

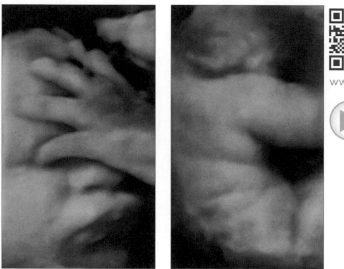

www.tyndal.es/twwyweek37

This baby looks as if he's wondering how much longer it will be until he can come out and get on with his life. The full, pouting mouth may be a reaction to the fact that he just poked himself in the eye with his chubby pinkie finger. You can see the umbilical cord just beneath his chin. In the second image, look at the rolls of fat around baby's midsection. Little love handles in the making.

# Development

By week thirty-seven, if I'm Caucasian, my eyes are probably blue. If I'm African American or Asian, my eyes are probably lighter than they will be about a month after birth. I'm recording memories by now, and I may soon drop or put my head in the pelvis area near the birth canal. This could cause you some discomfort. The bones in my head are still soft and pliable; this allows them to compress a little bit as I prepare to travel through your birth canal. This is also why I have a soft spot on top of my head for several months after I'm born.

# Rx for Health

By now, you might be experiencing the normal discomfort of pregnancy. First-time moms may feel the baby engaging in the pelvis or dropping about now. If this isn't your first delivery, your baby may not drop until labor. Sleeping may become more difficult due to discomfort. Some potential relief measures may be swimming, sleeping in a recliner, and frequent position changes. Low-back pain is also common. Your health-care provider may recommend some specific stretches to improve your symptoms.

**NUTRITIONAL NUGGET**
You can practically see the finish line from here. It's especially important to keep up good nutrition habits. Because of baby's size, your stomach cannot hold as much, and it empties fast. Some women late in their third trimester even begin to feel nausea and symptoms associated with the morning sickness they felt early in their pregnancies. If this happens, revisit some of the remedies that helped you then, but don't give in to the urge to reach for sugary or starchy snacks with no nutritional value. Instead, concentrate on small, frequent meals packed with vitamins and minerals.

## MOMMY MOMENTS
### Labor Day

Whether it starts gradually and builds or comes upon you suddenly, it's a day that will live in infamy. There are moments and conversations from our labor days and nights that we'll never forget. Here are just a few of them:

*We had just finished our Lamaze class and were taking a tour of the hospital when I felt like I had wet my pants. I asked our instructor to please explain again the difference between a trickle and a gush. Sure enough, my water had broken.* —HEATHER ENGLAND

*We were at the hardware store because my husband wanted to buy a mop to scrub the floors before the baby was born. That's where my water broke. We rushed to the hospital, leaving a need for cleanup on aisle 4!* —LAURA BOWLING

*With my second son, I had been induced, and the contractions were coming fast and furious. The nurse had left the room to go order my epidural, and as I was waiting, my husband climbed up beside me, smiled, and said, "Quickie?" It made me laugh and relax enough to make it till the drugs got there.* —CINDI CHIEN

*I was at the hospital, and when my baby's head was almost out, the doctor said, "Sit up and give me your hands." I thought it was just part of the birthing plan. He put my hands around Parker's shoulders, and I lifted him out! I laid him on my stomach in disbelief and amazement. I will always cherish that moment.* —MICHELLE GERHART

# PRENATAL POSTCARD

## Express Male by Jennifer Robinson

By baby number three, you think you've seen and done it all. I was dragging around a four-year-old and an almost-two-year-old. Life was pretty busy.

We were at my daughter's dance studio for class. When I stood up, I felt something a little wet and warm. I just assumed I'd had another "pregnancy moment," a frequent occurrence when I would cough, laugh, or do anything else too abruptly. It was just a drop or two, no biggie. So I loaded the kids in the car and headed out for our next stop, the post office.

It was April 14, and I knew the post office would be busy the next day with people mailing their taxes. I thought I'd beat the rush and mark the errand off my list. When I parked and stepped out of the SUV, it was more than a little oops or accident. My brand-new maternity capris were instantly wet to the knees. But I still quickly mailed the envelope and then climbed back in the SUV to call my husband.

Our premature son was born two days later on April 16. Wouldn't it have been wonderful if Uncle Sam had picked up the hospital bill for us? A girl can dream . . .

## "THANK YOU"

*I might not always remember everything you did to get me here . . . . to help me live. I know you thought of me each day for nine months. To carry me through, you must love me a bunch. Thanks for feeding me. Caring. Sharing your body. You still loved me, Mom, even when I caused you pain. I depend on you for everything. Later it'll be different but somehow the same. For all that you've done for me, for every-thing you'll do, from this small baby to my mommy, I want to say, "Thank you."*

## BABY NOTES

Have you had any baby showers? If so, name a few of the gifts you received. Who attended your shower?

........................................................................

........................................................................

........................................................................

........................................................................

........................................................................

........................................................................

........................................................................

........................................................................

........................................................................

# week THIRTY-EIGHT

Most babies are born within two weeks of their actual due date

# week THIRTY-EIGHT

### I'M THIS BIG: I'm nineteen and a half inches long, and I weigh six and a half pounds.

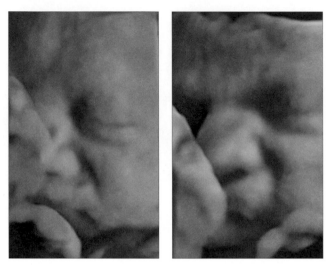

www.tyndal.es/twwyweek38

Aren't you glad that babies aren't claustrophobic? Living space couldn't get much tighter. This baby's nose is smashed up against the placenta. Look at those little lips! Sometimes your health-care provider can't tell baby's position from just feeling. He or she may order a sonogram just to determine whether the head is down. If baby isn't head down by this point, you can see why the close quarters make it difficult to turn.

# Development

By week thirty-eight, much of the vernix that once protected my skin has rubbed off. I'm no longer pressed into your rib cage. My body is usually plump. I've also shed most of the lanugo hair that covered my body. If you're having contractions, I can usually feel them. A change in hormones will trigger my release.

# Rx for Health

Every mom whose birth isn't scheduled wonders when it will be time to go to the hospital. The average mom can wait until her contractions are painful, and last for a minute, and come every five to seven minutes for at least an hour. If you think your water has broken, it's best to contact your health-care provider for advice.

**NUTRITIONAL NUGGET**
Labor and delivery put huge physical demands on your body—and on your baby. There are a few things you can do nutritionally to prepare.

If your body is giving you signs that labor may come soon, avoid gassy foods and don't eat a big meal. Instead, try easily digestible complex carbohydrates that provide long-term energy that you might need for labor. The body usually naturally clears itself out before the baby is born.

If you have a planned C-section, doctors usually don't want you to eat anything for six hours prior to surgery.

# MOMMY MOMENTS
## The Miracle of Motherhood

It's not just your body that has morphed during this nine-month journey. Your heart has probably evolved as well. Motherhood is one of the biggest changes in a woman's life. For a few years, you're given the responsibility not just of giving another person life but of nurturing his or her body, mind, and soul. It's definitely life altering for the giver.

*I was scared when I found out I was pregnant. I didn't want to have any children. Even the day I walked into the hospital, I didn't want to be a mother. But when I held my son and looked at him, he was absolutely perfect. I didn't know I could love so much. I wasn't a natural mother, but my son made me a mother. I'm more emotional now and more affectionate.* —BECKY MORRELL

*Pregnancy and the process of becoming a mother have changed me in so many ways. I have learned to rely more on God's grace rather than my own strength. I'm learning to be more laid-back, and I have a better perspective on what's important in life. It's really not all about me!* —ELLEN BRETH

*My priorities have changed. The day Gabby was born (six weeks early), I was supposed to be in Florida for a management assessment for work. I went from planning on going back to work full-time to thinking,* I can't leave this baby with anyone else. *If you ask any of my family, they will tell you they always thought I would be a career woman, moving up within a company. It's still hard to believe I became a stay-at-home mom.* —WYNNE COLEMAN

# PRENATAL POSTCARD

## The Angel of Faith by Mandy Powell

Doctors told me (and statistics agreed) that my twin girls only had a small chance of being born alive. I know now that steep odds are what miracles are made of.

My pregnancy was filled with problems from the beginning. At seven weeks, doctors told us our baby had no heartbeat. Two weeks later, our doctor looked up from the ultrasound screen and said, "Did we know you were having twins?"

At fifteen weeks, frequent, mild contractions began. By twenty-two weeks, I was in full labor. An ambulance rushed me to the hospital, where I was prepared to deliver babies too young to survive. Good doctors tried everything to stop my contractions. Finally they shook their heads and walked away, leaving nature to take its course.

Devastated, I prayed and put my girls in God's hands. And then Faith walked through my hospital door. She was an auburn-haired, middle-aged nurse whose very name comforted me through my first twelve hours of what would become fourteen weeks of bed rest. She competently monitored my vital signs and helped calm the raging side effects of the medication given to stop the contractions. And then she left.

After that first night, I knew whatever happened, God was in control.

Several weeks into my hospital stay, my new nurse said, "Wendy came by today to see how you were doing."

"Who is Wendy?" I asked.

"She was your nurse the night you were admitted."

"No, her name was Faith," I said.

"No, her name is Wendy," she replied.

"Which one was Faith?" I asked.

"There is no nurse by the name of Faith in OB, nor has there been since I've worked here."

I told the nurse my story about the comfort I received from Faith the first night, and she got chills on her arms, and tears filled her eyes.

My girls made it to thirty-six weeks. They were small but healthy. I no longer put limits on what God can do.

I never saw Faith again, but her caring vigil on my darkest night left me with a light that still illuminates my trust in God's miraculous love.

# A MIRACLE

*It's a miracle. I'm a miracle. It's true. Look at me. Look how complex I am. I have fingers and toes . . . two eyes and a nose. I have eyelashes and a chin . . . thoughts and feelings of my own. I'm a little person full of promise and possibility. I get to make decisions—just small ones at first. But soon they'll get bigger . . . like me. It's hard to believe all this came from two cells. Me! But I do believe in miracles because I felt it happen. Saw my first one right here in the dark. And this is only the beginning.*

## BABY NOTES

Write out a letter to your baby in anticipation of meeting him or her!

...............................................................................................

...............................................................................................

...............................................................................................

...............................................................................................

...............................................................................................

...............................................................................................

...............................................................................................

...............................................................................................

...............................................................................................

# week THIRTY-NINE

Baby's head may be bearing down on your cervix, causing it to thin

# week THIRTY-NINE

## I'M THIS BIG: I'm twenty inches long, and I weigh seven pounds.

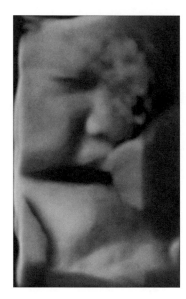

www.tyndal.es/twwyweek39

Look at the chub on this baby's chest and stomach. The left side of baby's face is pressed into Mom's uterine wall. It's sometimes hard to capture good ultrasound images of babies this close to delivery because the amniotic fluid is reduced and the baby is so big. This little one, with eyes squeezed shut, seems ready and waiting. Baby's head may be bearing down on your cervix, causing it to thin. Technically, this is the first stage of labor, which can last for days!

# Development

At thirty-nine weeks, I may come out anytime now. On average, I could weigh between five and a half and nine pounds and measure between seventeen and twenty-two inches. If I'm a boy, I usually weigh more than the girls. If I'm a second child, I usually weigh more than your first. Believe it or not, my fingernails may need to be trimmed.

# Rx for Health

There are numerous myths about how to stimulate labor at home. Castor oil, for instance, has been suggested for years. But it won't induce labor; it will only give you intestinal cramps and diarrhea. One possible method of natural induction is sex. Semen has chemicals that may stimulate uterine contractions, but only if the body is ready for labor.

**NUTRITIONAL NUGGET**
Some health-care providers encourage you to drink and eat light foods during labor, while others ban it. If there's a possibility that you'll need anesthesia for a surgical procedure, doctors don't want you to eat because it could cause you to vomit. That can cause big problems. If everything is progressing normally, a little snack and some fluid might energize you.

Just ask your health-care provider what he or she recommends in regard to eating or drinking. Some women munch on ice chips!

## MOMMY MOMENTS

### The Light at the End of the Tunnel

At the end of almost any natural labor and delivery comes the defining moment. Baby's head is pushed from darkness into light. It's the end and the beginning all rolled into one.

*When the nurse said, "I can see the head," she also said, "Stop pushing so I can run to get the doctor." Have you ever tried to stop pushing once the baby is there?* —SUSAN GIMOTTY

*I thought,* Thank the Lord! *I was so tired and just wanted it to be over.* —SARA LISSAUER

*When the doctor said, "I can see the head," I thought,* Are they lying to me to keep my spirits up? —ROBERTA SIMPSON

*I was confused and said, "My head? Oh, you see Brandon's head! Well, go get it. Get him out!"* —CELESTE KIRMER

*The doctor told me she could see the head. Two more pushes and my son Nicholas emerged. The doctor immediately placed him in my arms and I thought,* Of course you are my son. —JUNE SANTIAGO

# Prenatal Postcard

## Welcome to Walmart
## Marsheanna Clark's Story

I'd had a baby before, but it was nothing like this. About three o'clock one morning in early December, excruciating pain shot through my lower back. At thirty-nine weeks pregnant, I didn't recognize this as labor, and apparently neither did the emergency-room doctor. He just sent me home.

- Later that evening, I was feeling better and needing groceries, so my mom and I went to Walmart. Standing in the checkout line, I felt a trickle. And then a gush. The lady in front of me freaked out and ran away yelling. We stayed in line and paid for our groceries. I knew I was in labor. But these things usually take time.

As I walked out the door, the night air hit me in the face. I bent over. Impossible. I needed to push. The Salvation Army bell ringer knew something was wrong. She put her coat around me. A security officer and father of four pulled up a bench. I lay down, and the bell ringer held up a sheet. Scared and little embarrassed, I couldn't believe this was happening.

But I didn't have long to think on it, because I could now feel my baby's head. My sweatpants came off, and I said, "Mama, catch her!" And she did. Just like that, six pounds and seven ounces of baby girl was laid on my chest. And then the ambulance pulled up. They cracked a warm pack, spread a paper-thin blanket over us, and took us to the hospital, where they officially cut the cord on my healthy baby girl.

A couple of days later, the security officer and his wife gave me a Walmart gift card. The employees at the store adopted us for Christmas and sent us a few baby items we didn't have. As for me, if I ever get pregnant again, starting at about thirty-six weeks, I'm just going to sit down.

# READY OR NOT

*Are you ready, Mom? Is your bag packed? Is my nursery done? Do I have a diaper bag? Remember, Mom, to get our jammies . . . some for me and some for you. And don't forget to call my grammy. She'll want to be there too. Grab Dad and maybe a cab. It's the middle of the night. Turn out the lights. It really doesn't matter if you're ready or you're not. I'm getting pretty excited, so just take what we've got. And let's go!*

## BABY NOTES

Baby will be here soon. What still needs to be done before he or she arrives? Do you feel ready to meet your little one?

..............................................................................................

..............................................................................................

..............................................................................................

..............................................................................................

..............................................................................................

..............................................................................................

..............................................................................................

..............................................................................................

# week
# FORTY

It's time for baby to make his or her grand appearance!

# week FORTY

**I'M THIS BIG:** I'm twenty and a half inches long, and I weigh about seven and a half pounds.

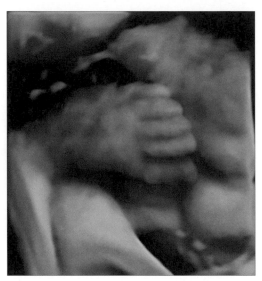

www.tyndal.es/twwyweek40

Baby is so smashed, he may not get his foot out of his face until he's born. There's just not much room for movement. You can see the loops of the umbilical cord wrapping under his chin and up over his foot. Labor can also be a bit uncomfortable for the baby as he or she moves into the birth canal. Baby releases large amounts of adrenaline. This keeps the heart pumping fast. Sonographers are sometimes asked to monitor baby by ultrasound during labor. Curious about what your baby is doing during a contraction? He or she is usually quiet and compressed with little movement because the fluid is gone from the uterus during heavy labor. Minutes before baby's debut, Mommy is doing most of the hard work.

# DEVELOPMENT

By forty weeks, I'm supposed to make my grand entrance, but it may take me as long as two more weeks. When I'm born, I see bright lights for the first time. I hear sounds no longer muffled by the buffer of your uterus. I take my first breath of cold air. I make my first audible sound, usually a cry. I may be a little swollen from my journey through the birth canal. My head may be a little cone-shaped. I'm usually hungry. I need a hug, some food, and a nap.

# RX FOR HEALTH

If you haven't gone into labor or delivered by this stage in your pregnancy, your health-care provider may talk to you about induction. Sometimes after week forty, amniotic-fluid levels decrease or your baby's growth is restricted, indicating that the placenta's function may be deteriorating. If that happens, baby isn't able to get enough nutrition or blood flow, and induced labor is suggested. Baby's increasing size may be another reason for induction. If baby is more than ten pounds, he or she may be too big to pass through the birth canal without damage. Your health-care provider may order a sonogram to determine if any of these factors exist.

**NUTRITIONAL NUGGET**
If you've had a normal vaginal delivery, dietitians say, "Let your hunger be your guide" on how much you should eat postbirth. Some women are very hungry; some are too exhausted to eat. You do need plenty of fluids to rehydrate. If you've delivered by C-section, you'll probably be on a soft diet until you're able to pass gas, which is a sign that your digestive system may be ready for something more substantial.

## MOMMY MOMENTS

### "The First Time Ever I Saw Your Face"

A baby's birth is more than just the emotional culmination of hormones, labor, and pain. It's the end of months of waiting. The fulfillment of years of dreaming. And it's the gift of one of life's dearest bonds.

*I cried, "He's beautiful."* —NOREEN DUPRIEST

*The first thing I said was, "Look how little she is!" My daughter weighed just over seven pounds, but my firstborn son was ten pounds!* —CAROL SUE WICKERSHAM

*They say babies don't come with instructions, but as our first baby was emerging from the birth canal, I heard God whisper,* You have been living for yourself. Now you must live for this child . . . and for Me. *It was a holy moment. God was there, attending the birth of my daughter, and He knew this mother needed instruction.* —SUZANNE FIELD

*I was really at a loss for words. It's awesome to know that I worked with God in creating a miracle.* —TRACY MCMINN

*They placed my son, Cyrus, on my chest and both my husband and I started crying. I said, "Hi, baby," and just felt flooded with emotion.* —SHERILYN SMITH

# PRENATAL POSTCARD

## Better Late by Jennifer Leiker

My husband and I always wanted children. We tried for years to conceive. We took every test. There was no medical reason for our infertility. After seventeen years of marriage, I missed a period. At forty-three, I thought my missed cycle was the start of menopause, not an answer to prayer. It took nearly the nine months to believe we were having a baby.

For the first two months, my husband, Danny, and I could barely make eye contact without tears welling up. When the numbness finally faded, we couldn't contain our excitement. We viewed this as a miracle baby. Family and friends admitted they had given up hope that we would ever have children.

Tears of joy streamed down my face when I saw Baby Janey for the first time. Years of buried emotions burst out. I never experienced anything that deeply before. My new sense of responsibility hit me with force. It was no longer just about me and Danny. I also experienced an immediate deeper love for my husband. He looked after Janey and me in a way I had never seen before. I know now there is nothing my husband wouldn't do for us.

After we brought Janey home, we began to notice her mannerisms were familiar. She was doing the same things we saw her doing in her 3-D sonograms. Months earlier, we spent more than an hour trying to get good images of her face. She kept her hands or feet in front of her the whole time. Janey still constantly has her hands in her face . . . awake or asleep.

## "MY BIRTHDAY"

*Today's the day. Yippee! Hurray! There's a change coming on. It's about time, I must say. We've waited so long. Was that tight squeeze my first hug? Or a contraction telling me to budge? Okay. I'm going. Will this hurt really bad? It better not. I'll tell my dad. Ouch! I'm moving, but it's tight in here. My head is smooshed. What was that? A cheer? For me? Because you can see . . . what?* Pop! *Out comes my face. Now I can see too. What a blurry, strange place. Push. There comes the rest. I'm pretty tired, but this is the best. I feel strong hands, a nurse, my dad. This is the first day I've ever had. They are picking me up to bring me to you. Let's cry now, Mom. We deserve it. Whew!*

## BABY NOTES

Describe your baby's birth physically and emotionally. What were your first thoughts or words to your baby?

..................................................................................

..................................................................................

..................................................................................

..................................................................................

..................................................................................

..................................................................................

..................................................................................

# week
# FORTY-
# ONE PLUS

Good things come to
those who wait

# week FORTY-ONE PLUS

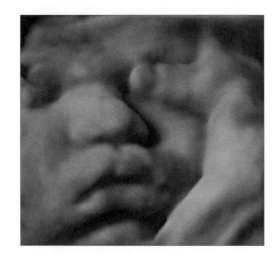

www.tyndal.es/twwyweek41

This little girl looks so peaceful, why would she want to leave? But Mom is usually more than ready for baby's arrival by this point. The mother's doctor ordered this ultrasound to check on baby's well-being. A sonographer can measure fluid levels and make sure baby is moving normally. That indicates that baby is still getting enough oxygen and nutrition from the placenta, and everything is still functioning well. If not, your health-care provider may want to induce labor to give baby his or her eviction notice.

# Development

I am fully developed, but not considered overdue until forty-two weeks. My vernix is probably wearing off and may expose my skin to the amniotic fluid. If that happens, my skin may become a little flakey. If your placenta is still functioning properly, I'm getting heavier.

# Rx for Health

Health-care providers don't always agree on when to induce labor when babies are overdue. The first step is as simple as checking the cervix. If you're not dilated and your cervix isn't thinning, inducing labor can increase the risk for a C-section. At that point, you'll probably need some tests to make sure baby is still doing well. Tests include assessment of the placenta and amniotic fluid levels by ultrasound, a check of fetal kick counts, and maybe a nonstress test, where a monitor is hooked up to your belly. If any of these are abnormal, it's best to get baby out.

**NUTRITIONAL NUGGET**
Remember, if you breast-feed your baby, you'll burn approximately five hundred additional calories a day. You need to keep up with your healthy diet, stay on your prenatal vitamins, and increase your fluids. The average baby drinks about twenty-three ounces of breast milk per day,[1] so you need to be drinking about thirteen eight-ounce cups of liquid every day. This includes water and other beverages (milk, juice, etc.).[2]

# MOMMY MOMENTS

## Being Overdue

Being overdue is tough emotionally and often physically as well. Some moms want to wait, while others are ready for help getting baby to move out.

> *Kelsy was three weeks late. I was miserable. My water finally broke around two o'clock one morning. Big shock, she was a bit overbaked. She had a full head of hair and long fingernails and had gone potty inside before she was delivered. What a crazy time. But she was absolutely beautiful and worth all the effort.* —KARLA SHOTTS

> *I was planning to have a home birth, and my baby was overdue. I was getting anxious that he wouldn't come. One day felt like a week. I had prepared my home, and my family was just waiting to come. I wasn't worried about the baby, but I could hardly stand to wait anymore.* —SHEILA HOWE

> *I went past my due date by a week. I worked full-time all the way to the last minute. I remember just kind of assuming every day when I left work that I wouldn't be back the next day. And then every morning, I'd wake up and I'd have to go to work!* —TRICIA CAMBRON

# PRENATAL POSTCARD

## To Those Who Wait by Lynne Carols

I was one of those women who knew exactly when I got pregnant. We were trying, so from the moment of conception, I was on a countdown. I actually marked days off a pregnancy calendar and scheduled my life accordingly. I set goals backward based on my due date. Like clockwork, I had the nursery done on time. The baby clothes from baby showers were washed in special detergent and hung delicately in the closet. I stacked tiny diapers in a basket on the changing table. My bag was packed. My plans were laid.

My husband's parents came into town to watch my three-year-old the day before my due date. I'm telling you, we were ready with a capital R!

On D-day there was one problem. Failure to launch. After three days, my countdown was an epic fail. My biologically synchronized watch practically had the springs sticking out. We had nothing to do but stare at my baby bump and will it to give way. My doctor said we should wait at least a week before scheduling a sonogram to check on baby's well-being. I knew another week would push my precariously balanced bulge right over the edge.

By day four, I was researching natural ways to move the process along. I tried the ones I could stomach, to no avail. So I walked . . . everywhere. In my big mama voice I used my baby's first, middle, and last name to order him out. He was having none of it. After a three-mile jaunt around the neighborhood, I fell into bed exhausted. Mentally. Physically. Prenatally.

And then, sometime in the wee hours of day five, it happened. The blessed contractions that move us all from darkness into light. The gentle push that turns into a mighty rush. Just like that. Labor moved me from a forty-one-week waiting room to the delivery room. And it's absolutely true that good things come to those who wait.

# SEE YOU SOON!

*I know you're anxious and ready to meet me, Mom. Don't worry! It won't be long now. I'm ready to cuddle up against you and feel your arms around me. I love you already.*

## BABY NOTES

Explain your feelings about being overdue.

.................................................................................

.................................................................................

.................................................................................

.................................................................................

.................................................................................

.................................................................................

.................................................................................

.................................................................................

.................................................................................

.................................................................................

.................................................................................

.................................................................................

# Notes

**WEEK TWO**

1. Centers for Disease Control and Prevention, "Folic Acid: Recommendations," January 13, 2012, http://www.cdc.gov/ncbddd/folicacid/recommendations .html.
2. Institute of Medicine, Food and Nutrition Board, *Dietary Reference Intakes for Thiamin, Riboflavin, Niacin, Vitamin B6, Folate, Vitamin B12, Pantothenic Acid, Biotin, and Choline* (Washington, DC: National Academies Press, 1998), 566–567, http://www.nap.edu/openbook.php?record_id=6015&page=566.
3. Centers for Disease Control and Prevention, "CDC Grand Rounds: Additional Opportunities to Prevent Neural Tube Defects with Folic Acid Fortification," *Morbidity and Mortality Weekly Report* 59, no. 31 (August 2010): 980–984, http://www.cdc.gov/mmwr/preview/mmwrhtml/mm5931a2.htm.

**WEEK THREE**

1. Institute of Medicine, *Dietary Reference Intakes: The Essential Guide to Nutrient Requirements,* eds. Jennifer J. Otten, Jennifer Pitzi Hellwig, and Linda D. Meyers (Washington, DC: National Academies Press, 2006), 144, 244, 328, http://www.iom.edu/Reports/2006/Dietary-Reference-Intakes -Essential-Guide-Nutrient-Requirements.aspx.
2. Ibid., 286.
3. Eileen R. Fowles, "What's a Pregnant Woman to Eat: A Review of Current USDA Dietary Guidelines and MyPyramid," *Journal of Perinatal Education* 15, no. 4 (Fall 2006): 28–33, http://www.ncbi.nlm.nih.gov/pmc/articles /PMC1876595/.
4. Study conducted by Monika Lukesch, Constantine University, Frankfurt, Germany, cited in Thomas Verny, *The Secret Life of the Unborn Child: How You Can Prepare Your Baby for a Happy, Healthy Life* (New York: Dell, 1981).

**WEEK FOUR**

1. Baby measurements and weights for each week of pregnancy are based on approximations. Since every baby develops differently, a perfectly normal newborn can weigh five pounds or eleven pounds. Data taken from Peter M. Doubilet et al., "Improved Birth Weight Table for Neonates Developed from Gestations Dated by Early Ultrasonography," *Journal of Ultrasound Medicine* 16, no. 4 (April 1997): 241; Frank P. Hadlock et al., "Fetal Crown Rump Length: Reevaluation of Relation to Menstrual Age with High Resolution Real-Time," *US Radiology* 182, no. 2 (February 1992): 501; R. Usher and

F. McLean, "Intrauterine Growth of Live-Born Caucasian Infants at Sea Level: Standards Obtained from Measurements in Seven Dimensions of Infants Born between Twenty-Five and Forty-Four Weeks of Gestation," *Journal of Pediatrics* 74, no. 6 (June 1969); F. Gary Cunningham et al., *Williams Obstetrics*, 23rd ed. (New York: McGraw-Hill, 2010).

2. According to the Institute of Medicine, the upper intake level for pregnant and lactating women over the age of eighteen is 2,500 mg. See Catharine A. Ross et al., *Dietary Reference Intakes for Calcium and Vitamin D* (Washington, DC: Institute of Medicine, 2010), 2, http://www.iom.edu/~/media/Files/Report%20Files/2010/Dietary-Reference-Intakes-for-Calcium-and-Vitamin-D/Vitamin%20D%20and%20Calcium%202010%20Report%20Brief.pdf.

**WEEK FIVE**

1. Terry J. DuBose, *Fetal Sonography* (St. Louis, MO: W. B. Saunders, 1996), 258.
2. Ibid., 266–269.
3. Theresa O. Scholl et al., "Low Zinc Intake during Pregnancy: Its Association with Preterm and Very Preterm Delivery," *American Journal of Epidemiology* 137, no. 10 (May 1993): 1115–1124.
4. Institute of Medicine, Food and Nutrition Board, *Dietary Reference Intakes for Vitamin A, Vitamin K, Arsenic, Boron, Chromium, Copper, Iodine, Iron, Manganese, Molybdenum, Nickel, Silicon, Vanadium, and Zinc* (Washington, DC: National Academy Press, 2001), 772–773, http://www.nap.edu/openbook.php?record_id=10026&page=R2.
5. Brady E. Hamilton et al., "Births: Preliminary Data for 2011," *National Vital Statistics Reports* 61, no. 5 (October 2012); Gretchen Livingston and D'Vera Cohn, "US Birth Rate Falls to a Record Low: Decline Is Greatest among Immigrants," *Social and Demographic Trends* (Washington, DC: Pew Research Center, 2012): 1, 3, http://www.pewsocialtrends.org/files/2012/11/Birth_Rate_Final.pdf.
6. National Center for Health Statistics, "Provisional Monthly and Twelve-Month Ending Number of Live Births, Deaths, and Infant Deaths and Rates: United States, January 2011–December 2012," Centers for Disease Control and Prevention, http://www.cdc.gov/nchs/data/dvs/provisional_tables/Provisional_Table01_2012Dec.pdf.
7. Joyce A. Martin et al., "Births: Final Data for 2011," *National Vital Statistics Reports* 62, no. 1 (June 2013): 3, http://www.cdc.gov/nchs/data/nvsr/nvsr62/nvsr62_01.pdf.
8. Ibid., 7.
9. Ibid., "Table 12: Birth Rates, by Age of Mother: United States, Each State and Territory, 2011," 40.

**WEEK SIX**

1. Institute of Medicine, *Dietary Reference Intakes: The Essential Guide to Nutrient Requirements*, eds. Jennifer J. Otten, Jennifer Pitzi Hellwig, and

Linda D. Meyers (Washington, DC: National Academies Press, 2006), 170,
http://www.nap.edu/catalog/11537.html.

**WEEK SEVEN**
1. Cited in James A. Greenberg, Stacey J. Bell, and Wendy van Ausdal,
   "Omega-3 Fatty Acid Supplementation during Pregnancy," *Obstetrics and
   Gynecology* 1, no. 4 (Fall 2008): 162–169, http://www.ncbi.nlm.nih.gov/pmc
   /articles/PMC2621042/.
2. "Pregnancy," InnerBody.com, http://www.innerbody.com/image/repo11
   .html.

**WEEK EIGHT**
1. Institute of Medicine, *Dietary Reference Intakes: The Essential Guide to
   Nutrient Requirements*, eds. Jennifer J. Otten, Jennifer Pitzi Hellwig, and
   Linda D. Meyers (Washington, DC: National Academies Press, 2006), 144,
   http://www.nap.edu/openbook.php?record_id=11537&page=144.
2. Linda E. May et al., "Aerobic Exercise during Pregnancy Influences Fetal
   Cardiac Autonomic Control of Heart Rate and Heart Rate Variability," *Early
   Human Development* 86, no. 4 (April 2010): 213–17, http://www.sciencedirect
   .com/science/article/pii/S0378378210000617.

**WEEK ELEVEN**
1. Institute of Medicine, *Dietary Reference Intakes: The Essential Guide to
   Nutrient Requirements*, eds. Jennifer J. Otten, Jennifer Pitzi Hellwig, and
   Linda D. Meyers (Washington, DC: National Academies Press, 2006), 328,
   http://www.nap.edu/openbook.php?record_id=11537&page=328.
2. American College of Obstetricians and Gynecologists, "Car Safety for You
   and Your Baby," FAQ018, August 2011, http://www.acog.org/~/media/For
   %20Patients/faq018.pdf?dmc=1&ts=20131106T1355030853; "Travel During
   Pregnancy," FAQ055, August 2011, http://www.acog.org/~/media/For%20
   Patients/faq055.pdf?dmc=1&ts=20131106T1358278686.

**WEEK TWELVE**
1. Institute of Medicine, *Dietary Reference Intakes: The Essential Guide to
   Nutrient Requirements*, eds. Jennifer J. Otten, Jennifer Pitzi Hellwig, and
   Linda D. Meyers (Washington, DC: National Academies Press, 2006), 157,
   http://www.nap.edu/openbook.php?record_id=11537&page=157.
2. Endowment for Human Development, *The Biology of Prenatal Development*
   (DVD), 2006; "Movie Theater: Reflexive Movement," http://www.ehd.org
   /movies.php?mov_id=47.

**WEEK FOURTEEN**
1. Committee on Obstetric Practice, "Moderate Caffeine Consumption during
   Pregnancy," *American College of Obstetricians and Gynecologists Committee*

*Opinion*, no. 462, August 2010, http://www.acog.org/Resources%20And%20
Publications/Committee%20Opinions/Committee%20on%20Obstetric%20
Practice/Moderate%20Caffeine%20Consumption%20During%20Pregnancy
.aspx.
2. E. K. Ji et al., "Effects of Ultrasound on Maternal-Fetal Bonding: A Comparison
of Two- and Three-Dimensional Imaging," *Ultrasound in Obstetrics and
Gynecology* 25, no. 5 (May 2005): 473–477, http://onlinelibrary.wiley.com
/doi/10.1002/uog.1896/full.

**WEEK FIFTEEN**
1. Thorhallur I. Halldorsson et al., "Intake of Artificially Sweetened Soft
Drinks and Risk of Preterm Delivery: A Prospective Cohort Study in 59,334
Danish Pregnant Women" *American Journal of Clinical Nutrition* 92, no. 3
(September 2010): 626–633, http://ajcn.nutrition.org/content/92/3/626
.abstract.

**WEEK SIXTEEN**
1. Kathleen A. Costigan, Heather L. Sipsma, and Janet A. DiPietro, "Pregnancy
Folklore Revisited: The Case of Heartburn and Hair," *Birth* 33, no. 4
(December 2006): 311–14, http://onlinelibrary.wiley.com/doi/10.1111
/j.1523-536X.2006.00128.x/abstract.
2. Audrey F. Saftlas et al., "Does Chocolate Intake during Pregnancy Reduce
the Risks of Preeclampsia and Gestational Hypertension?" *Annals of
Epidemiology* 20, no. 8 (August 2010): 584–91, http://www.ncbi.nlm.nih
.gov/pmc/articles/PMC2901253/.

**WEEK SEVENTEEN**
1. Neil A. Segal et al., "Pregnancy Leads to Lasting Changes in Foot Structure,"
*American Journal of Physical Medicine and Rehabilitation* 92, no. 3 (March
2013): 232–240, http://www.ncbi.nlm.nih.gov/pubmed/23117270.

**WEEK EIGHTEEN**
1. Martin Witt and Klaus Reutter, "Embryonic and Early Fetal Development of
Human Taste Buds: A Transmission Electron Microscopical Study," *Anatomical
Record* 246, no. 4 (December 1996): 507–523, http://onlinelibrary.wiley.com
/doi/10.1002/(SICI)1097-0185(199612)246:4%3C507::AID-AR10%3E3.0.CO;2
-S/abstract.
2. Studies cited in Janet L. Hopson, "Fetal Psychology," *Psychology Today*,
September 1, 1998, http://www.psychologytoday.com/articles/199809
/fetal-psychology.
3. National Library of Medicine, "Managing Your Weight Gain during
Pregnancy," MedlinePlus, National Institutes of Health, August 23, 2012,
http://www.nlm.nih.gov/medlineplus/ency/patientinstructions/000603.htm.

**WEEK NINETEEN**

1. Catharine A. Ross et al., "Dietary Reference Intakes for Calcium and Vitamin D," Institute of Medicine, November 2010, http://www.iom.edu/~/media/Files/Report%20Files/2010/Dietary-Reference-Intakes-for-Calcium-and-Vitamin-D/Vitamin%20D%20and%20Calcium%202010%20Report%20Brief.pdf.
2. T. J. Mathews and Brady E. Hamilton, "Trend Analysis of the Sex Ratio at Birth in the United States," *National Vital Statistics Reports* 53, no. 20 (June 2005), http://www.cdc.gov/nchs/data/nvsr/nvsr53/nvsr53_20.pdf.

**WEEK TWENTY**

1. Sarah J. Lewis et al., "Fetal Alcohol Exposure and IQ at Age Eight: Evidence from a Population-Based Birth-Cohort Study," *PLOS ONE* 7, no. 11 (September 2011), http://www.plosone.org/article/info%3Adoi%2F10.1371%2Fjournal.pone.0049407.
2. American College of Obstetricians and Gynecologists, "Tobacco, Alcohol, Drugs, and Pregnancy," FAQ170, Pregnancy, August 2011, http://www.acog.org/~/media/For%20Patients/faq170.pdf?dmc=1&ts=20130822T1904395514.
3. Janet L. Hopson, "Fetal Psychology," *Psychology Today*, September 1, 1998.

**WEEK TWENTY-TWO**

1. American College of Obstetrics and Gynecology, cited in Carrie Armstrong, "ACOG Guidelines on Psychiatric Medication Use during Pregnancy and Lactation," *American Family Physician* 78, no. 6 (September 2008): 772–778, Table 1, http://www.aafp.org/afp/2008/0915/p772.html.
2. David Chamberlain, *Babies Remember Birth* (New York: Ballantine Books, 1989), 44.

**WEEK TWENTY-SEVEN**

1. Food and Drug Administration and Environmental Protection Agency, "What You Need to Know about Mercury in Fish and Shellfish," pub. no. EPA-823-F-04-009, http://www.fda.gov/downloads/Food/FoodborneIllness Contaminants/UCM182158.pdf.
2. Ibid.
3. Sjurdur Frodi Olsen and Niels Jorgen Secher, "Low Consumption of Seafood in Early Pregnancy as a Risk Factor for Preterm Delivery: Prospective Cohort Study," *British Medical Journal* 324, no. 7335 (February 2002): 447–450.
4. Sunita R. Cheruku et al., "Higher Maternal Plasma Docosahexaenoic Acid during Pregnancy Is Associated with More Mature Neonatal Sleep-State Patterning," *American Journal of Clinical Nutrition* 76, no. 3 (September 2002): 608–613, http://ajcn.nutrition.org/content/76/3/608.full.

**WEEK TWENTY-NINE**

1. Institute of Medicine, *Dietary Reference Intakes: The Essential Guide to Nutrient Requirements*, eds. Jennifer J. Otten, Jennifer Pitzi Hellwig, and

Linda D. Meyers (Washington, DC: National Academies Press, 2006), 82, http://www.nap.edu/openbook.php?record_id=11537&page=82.

2. J. A. Mennella and G. K. Beauchamp, "The Early Development of Human Flavor Preferences," in *Why We Eat What We Eat: The Psychology of Eating,* ed. E. D. Capaldi (Washington, DC: American Psychological Association, 1996), 83–112.

**WEEK THIRTY-ONE**

1. Nadja Reissland, Brian Francis, and James Mason, "Development of Fetal Yawn Compared with Nonyawn Mouth Openings from Twenty-Four to Thirty-Six Weeks Gestation," *PLOS ONE* 7, no. 11 (November 2012), http://www.plosone.org/article/info:doi/10.1371/journal.pone.0050569?imageURI=info:doi/10.1371/journal.pone.0050569.g001.
2. Roseriet Beijers et al., "Maternal Prenatal Anxiety and Stress Predict Infant Illnesses and Health Complaints," *Pediatrics* 126, no. 2 (August 2010), http://pediatrics.aappublications.org/content/126/2/e401.full.pdf.
3. Visit www.stressfreestart.com to learn more about how you can reduce stress during pregnancy.

**WEEK THIRTY-TWO**

1. Carolyn Guenther Molloy, www.stressfreestart.com.

**WEEK THIRTY-THREE**

1. Research cited in David B. Chamberlain, "The Fetal Senses: A Classical View," *Life before Birth*, Birth Psychology.com, http://birthpsychology.com/free-article/fetal-senses-classical-view.
2. Howard P. Roffwarg, Joseph N. Muzio, and William C. Dement "Ontogenetic Development of the Human Sleep-Dream Cycle," *Science* 152, no. 3722 (April 1966): 604–619.

**WEEK THIRTY-FOUR**

1. John Colombo et al., "Maternal DHA and the Development of Attention in Infancy and Toddlerhood," *Child Development* 75, no. 4 (July/August 2004): 1254–1267, http://people.stfx.ca/x2009/x2009khe/DHA.pdf.
2. Rulla M. Tamimi et al., "Average Energy Intake among Pregnant Women Carrying a Boy Compared with a Girl," *British Medical Journal* 326, no. 7401 (June 2003): 1245–1246, http://www.ncbi.nlm.nih.gov/pmc/articles/PMC161555/.
3. Ibid.

**WEEK THIRTY-FIVE**

1. Rebecca Fischer's Sunflower Seed and Caramelized Onion Frittata recipe (http://kcwellnessguide.com)

2 tablespoons coconut oil or extra-virgin olive oil
1/2 sweet onion, thinly sliced
1 garlic clove, minced
2 cups chopped spinach
8 cage-free eggs
1/4 cup sunflower seeds
1/2 cup organic mozzarella cheese
Sea salt and white pepper, to taste

*Instructions:*
1. Preheat oven to 350 degrees Fahrenheit.
2. Heat 1 tablespoon oil in oven-safe skillet over low-medium heat. Add onion and cook for 5 to 10 minutes. Add garlic and cook for another minute.
3. Sprinkle with a couple of tablespoons of water, add the spinach, and cook for 2 minutes, stirring occasionally. Remove from stovetop and let cool.
4. In large bowl, whisk eggs together until fluffy and season with salt and pepper. Add sunflower seeds, mozzarella, and spinach mixture and stir to combine.
5. Heat remaining tablespoon of oil in skillet and add egg mixture. Cook for a few minutes, until edges turn white.
6. Move skillet to oven and bake for about 10 minutes, until eggs are fully cooked.
Makes three servings.

**WEEK THIRTY-SIX**
1. Institute of Medicine, *Dietary Reference Intakes: The Essential Guide to Nutrient Requirements*, eds. Jennifer J. Otten, Jennifer Pitzi Hellwig, and Linda D. Meyers (Washington, DC: National Academies Press, 2006), 340 http://www.nap.edu/openbook.php?record_id=11537&page=340.
2. Ibid., 402.
3. Eino Partanen et al., "Learning-induced Neural Plasticity of Speech Processing before Birth," *Proceedings of the National Academy of Sciences* 110, no. 37 (September 2013): 15145–15150, http://www.pnas.org/search?fulltext=Minna Huotilainen&submit=yes&x=0&y=0.
4. Minna Huotilainen, quoted in National Library of Medicine, "Babies May Remember Words Heard before Birth," MedlinePlus, National Institutes of Health, August 16, 2013, http://www.nlm.nih.gov/medlineplus/news/fullstory_140079.html.

**WEEK THIRTY-SEVEN**
1. Jennifer L. Bailit et al., "Maternal and Neonatal Outcomes by Labor Onset Type and Gestational Age," *American Journal of Obstetrics and Gynecology* 202, no. 3 (March 2010), http://www.ncbi.nlm.nih.gov/pmc/articles/PMC2888294/.

2. Research cited in March of Dimes, "Get Ready for Labor," http://www
.marchofdimes.com/pregnancy/why-at-least-39-weeks-is-best-for-your
-baby.aspx.
3. Bailit et al., "Maternal and Neonatal Outcomes," *Obstetrics and Gynecology*,
http://www.ncbi.nlm.nih.gov/pmc/articles/PMC2888294/.

**WEEK FORTY**
1. Anthony J. DeCasper and Ann D. Sigafoos, "The Intrauterine Heartbeat: A
Potent Reinforcer for Newborns," *Infant Behavior and Development* 6, no. 1
(1983): 19–25.

**WEEK FORTY-ONE PLUS**
1. Alan Greene, "Breast Milk in a Bottle," Parents, http://www.parents.com
/baby/feeding/bottlefeeding/breast-milk-in-a-bottle/.
2. Institute of Medicine, *Dietary Reference Intakes: The Essential Guide to
Nutrient Requirements*, eds. Jennifer J. Otten, Jennifer Pitzi Hellwig, and
Linda D. Meyers (Washington, DC: National Academies Press, 2006), 157,
http://www.nap.edu/openbook.php?record_id=11537&page=157.

# Your Pregnancy Calendar

*Hi, Mama-friend,*

*Pregnancy can be exciting, emotional, and exhausting. How can such a wee one shift your entire center of gravity in one tiny burst?*

*I know that little bun-in-the-oven just grew your to-do list by a mile. And you can almost hear the trimesters ticking away. But someday you are going to look back on your pregnancy and wonder where the time went. This calendar is to help you along. When you feel the baby kick but don't have time to journal about it, just grab a sticker and affix it to the date. Use it to help you remember appointments and record your moods, questions, and precious moments along the way.*

*Your due date is usually calculated using the first day of your last menstrual period. In other words, health-care providers start the countdown two weeks before you are actually pregnant . . . for a total of forty weeks.*

*To use the following calendar, take the first day of your last normal period and write it in as the first day of week one. Using this as your starting point, date the rest of your calendar. You may want to use a regular calendar to remind yourself which months have twenty-eight, thirty, and thirty-one days each. Do not skip any boxes.*

*There is a chance, if your periods are not regular, that you have no idea when you conceived. If that is the case, your health-care provider will probably order an ultrasound to help determine the due date. Remember, the earlier the ultrasound is done, the more accurately a sonographer can predict when baby will arrive. Keep in mind, your actual delivery date can vary from two weeks before to two weeks after your due date and still be considered normal.*

*I guarantee that in a few years when your life is busy with a whole new set of wonders, you will look back on this calendar and smile over things you might have forgotten. And one day in the fast-approaching future, your baby will be having a baby. And that boy or girl will have questions that only you can answer about his or her own beginnings. That is when you will pull out this pregnancy calendar again to connect and compare and reminisce. It will be like a time capsule containing a vintage reminder of your budding love for your child.*

*So let the journey of new life begin! I'm relishing every moment with you.*

*Your friend,*
*Carey Wickersham*

# WEEKS 1-4

Turn to pages 1–24 to see detailed information on the size and development of your baby, nutritional information for your health, and more.

| week 1 | | | | | | |
|---|---|---|---|---|---|---|
| ___/ | ___/ | ___/ | ___/ | ___/ | ___/ | ___/ |

| week 1 | | | | | | |
|---|---|---|---|---|---|---|
| ___/ | ___/ | ___/ | ___/ | ___/ | ___/ | ___/ |

| week 3 | | | | | | |
|---|---|---|---|---|---|---|
| ___/ | ___/ | ___/ | ___/ | ___/ | ___/ | ___/ |

| week 4 | | | | | | |
|---|---|---|---|---|---|---|
| ___/ | ___/ | ___/ | ___/ | ___/ | ___/ | ___/ |

NOTES ................................................................
................................................................
................................................................

# WEEKS 5-8

Turn to pages 25-48 to see detailed information on the size and development of your baby, nutritional information for your health, and more.

**week 5**

| / | / | / | / | / | / | / |
|---|---|---|---|---|---|---|
|   |   |   |   |   |   |   |

**week 6**

| / | / | / | / | / | / | / |
|---|---|---|---|---|---|---|
|   |   |   |   |   |   |   |

**week 7**

| / | / | / | / | / | / | / |
|---|---|---|---|---|---|---|
|   |   |   |   |   |   |   |

**week 8**

| / | / | / | / | / | / | / |
|---|---|---|---|---|---|---|
|   |   |   |   |   |   |   |

NOTES ..........................................................................................................

...........................................................................................................................

...........................................................................................................................

# WEEKS 9-12

Turn to pages 49–72 to see detailed information on the size and development of your baby, nutritional information for your health, and more.

**week 9**

___/___  ___/___  ___/___  ___/___  ___/___  ___/___  ___/___

**week 10**

___/___  ___/___  ___/___  ___/___  ___/___  ___/___  ___/___

**week 11**

___/___  ___/___  ___/___  ___/___  ___/___  ___/___  ___/___

**week 12**

___/___  ___/___  ___/___  ___/___  ___/___  ___/___  ___/___

NOTES ....................................................................................................

....................................................................................................

....................................................................................................

# WEEKS 13-16

Turn to pages 73-96 to see detailed information on the size and development of your baby, nutritional information for your health, and more.

**week 13**

___ / ___   ___ / ___   ___ / ___   ___ / ___   ___ / ___   ___ / ___   ___ / ___

**week 14**

___ / ___   ___ / ___   ___ / ___   ___ / ___   ___ / ___   ___ / ___   ___ / ___

**week 15**

___ / ___   ___ / ___   ___ / ___   ___ / ___   ___ / ___   ___ / ___   ___ / ___

**week 16**

___ / ___   ___ / ___   ___ / ___   ___ / ___   ___ / ___   ___ / ___   ___ / ___

NOTES ..............................................................................................................

........................................................................................................................

........................................................................................................................

# WEEKS 17-20

Turn to pages 97–120 to see detailed information on the size and development of your baby, nutritional information for your health, and more.

**week 17**

| / | / | / | / | / | / | / |
|---|---|---|---|---|---|---|
|   |   |   |   |   |   |   |

**week 18**

| / | / | / | / | / | / | / |
|---|---|---|---|---|---|---|
|   |   |   |   |   |   |   |

**week 19**

| / | / | / | / | / | / | / |
|---|---|---|---|---|---|---|
|   |   |   |   |   |   |   |

**week 20**

| / | / | / | / | / | / | / |
|---|---|---|---|---|---|---|
|   |   |   |   |   |   |   |

NOTES

..................................................................................................................

..................................................................................................................

..................................................................................................................

# WEEKS 21-24

Turn to pages 121–144 to see detailed information on the size and development of your baby, nutritional information for your health, and more.

**week 21**

| ___/___ | ___/___ | ___/___ | ___/___ | ___/___ | ___/___ | ___/___ |
|---|---|---|---|---|---|---|
| | | | | | | |

**week 22**

| ___/___ | ___/___ | ___/___ | ___/___ | ___/___ | ___/___ | ___/___ |
|---|---|---|---|---|---|---|
| | | | | | | |

**week 23**

| ___/___ | ___/___ | ___/___ | ___/___ | ___/___ | ___/___ | ___/___ |
|---|---|---|---|---|---|---|
| | | | | | | |

**week 24**

| ___/___ | ___/___ | ___/___ | ___/___ | ___/___ | ___/___ | ___/___ |
|---|---|---|---|---|---|---|
| | | | | | | |

NOTES ...........................................................................................................

............................................................................................................................

............................................................................................................................

# WEEKS 25-28

Turn to pages 145–168 to see detailed information on the size and development of your baby, nutritional information for your health, and more.

**week 25**

___ / ___ ___ / ___ ___ / ___ ___ / ___ ___ / ___ ___ / ___ ___ / ___

**week 26**

___ / ___ ___ / ___ ___ / ___ ___ / ___ ___ / ___ ___ / ___ ___ / ___

**week 27**

___ / ___ ___ / ___ ___ / ___ ___ / ___ ___ / ___ ___ / ___ ___ / ___

**week 28**

___ / ___ ___ / ___ ___ / ___ ___ / ___ ___ / ___ ___ / ___ ___ / ___

NOTES

# WEEKS 29-32

Turn to pages 169–192 to see detailed information on the size and development of your baby, nutritional information for your health, and more.

| week 29 | | | | | | |
|---|---|---|---|---|---|---|
| ___/ | ___/ | ___/ | ___/ | ___/ | ___/ | ___/ |

| week 30 | | | | | | |
|---|---|---|---|---|---|---|
| ___/ | ___/ | ___/ | ___/ | ___/ | ___/ | ___/ |

| week 31 | | | | | | |
|---|---|---|---|---|---|---|
| ___/ | ___/ | ___/ | ___/ | ___/ | ___/ | ___/ |

| week 32 | | | | | | |
|---|---|---|---|---|---|---|
| ___/ | ___/ | ___/ | ___/ | ___/ | ___/ | ___/ |

NOTES
.......................................................................................
.......................................................................................
.......................................................................................

# WEEKS 33-36

Turn to pages 193–216 to see detailed information on the size and development of your baby, nutritional information for your health, and more.

**week 33**

| ___/___ | ___/___ | ___/___ | ___/___ | ___/___ | ___/___ | ___/___ |
|---------|---------|---------|---------|---------|---------|---------|
|         |         |         |         |         |         |         |

**week 34**

| ___/___ | ___/___ | ___/___ | ___/___ | ___/___ | ___/___ | ___/___ |
|---------|---------|---------|---------|---------|---------|---------|
|         |         |         |         |         |         |         |

**week 35**

| ___/___ | ___/___ | ___/___ | ___/___ | ___/___ | ___/___ | ___/___ |
|---------|---------|---------|---------|---------|---------|---------|
|         |         |         |         |         |         |         |

**week 36**

| ___/___ | ___/___ | ___/___ | ___/___ | ___/___ | ___/___ | ___/___ |
|---------|---------|---------|---------|---------|---------|---------|
|         |         |         |         |         |         |         |

NOTES ...........................................................................

...................................................................................

...................................................................................

# WEEKS 37-40

Turn to pages 217–240 to see detailed information on the size and development of your baby, nutritional information for your health, and more.

**week 37**

| ___ / ___ | ___ / ___ | ___ / ___ | ___ / ___ | ___ / ___ | ___ / ___ | ___ / ___ |
|---|---|---|---|---|---|---|
|  |  |  |  |  |  |  |

**week 38**

| ___ / ___ | ___ / ___ | ___ / ___ | ___ / ___ | ___ / ___ | ___ / ___ | ___ / ___ |
|---|---|---|---|---|---|---|
|  |  |  |  |  |  |  |

**week 39**

| ___ / ___ | ___ / ___ | ___ / ___ | ___ / ___ | ___ / ___ | ___ / ___ | ___ / ___ |
|---|---|---|---|---|---|---|
|  |  |  |  |  |  |  |

**week 40**

| ___ / ___ | ___ / ___ | ___ / ___ | ___ / ___ | ___ / ___ | ___ / ___ | ___ / ___ |
|---|---|---|---|---|---|---|
|  |  |  |  |  |  |  |

NOTES .................................................................................................

.................................................................................................

.................................................................................................

# WEEKS 41-44

Turn to pages 241–246 to see detailed information on the size and development of your baby, nutritional information for your health, and more.

**week 41**

| ____ / ____ | ____ / ____ | ____ / ____ | ____ / ____ | ____ / ____ | ____ / ____ | ____ / ____ |
|---|---|---|---|---|---|---|
| | | | | | | |

**week 42**

| ____ / ____ | ____ / ____ | ____ / ____ | ____ / ____ | ____ / ____ | ____ / ____ | ____ / ____ |
|---|---|---|---|---|---|---|
| | | | | | | |

**week 43**

| ____ / ____ | ____ / ____ | ____ / ____ | ____ / ____ | ____ / ____ | ____ / ____ | ____ / ____ |
|---|---|---|---|---|---|---|
| | | | | | | |

**week 44**

| ____ / ____ | ____ / ____ | ____ / ____ | ____ / ____ | ____ / ____ | ____ / ____ | ____ / ____ |
|---|---|---|---|---|---|---|
| | | | | | | |

NOTES ........................................................................................................................

........................................................................................................................

........................................................................................................................

# PLANNED PARENTHOOD SELLING ABORTED BABY PARTS

"Less Crunchy": Another haggler in the PP meat market.

"We've been very good at getting heart, lung, liver... so I'm not gonna' crush that part. I'm gonna basically crush below; I'm gonna crush above; and I'm gonna see if I can get it all intact."

Planned Parenthood is a business-minded organization looking to make a profit.

Obama to Planned Parenthood: "Thank you—God bless you."

## PRESIDENT OBAMA STANDS WITH PLANNED PARENTHOOD

SHOCKING VIDEO CAUGHT ANOTHER TOP PLANNED PARENTHOOD DOCTOR SELLING BODY PARTS OF ABORTED BABIES

"It's been years since I've talked about compensation, so let me figure out what others are getting. If this is in the ballpark, it's fine. If it's still low, we can bump it up. I want a Lamborghini."

"Look at all this outrage over a dead lion, but where is all the outrage over the Planned Parenthood dead babies."
—**Marco Rubio**

"That many in the national media are more concerned with Cecil the lion than Planned Parenthood killing babies to harvest their organs is unconscionable."
—**Governor Mike Huckabee**

A bit
nervous

Hospital
tour

Prenatal
class

Prenatal
class

Good-bye
2nd trimester,
hello 3rd!

Positive
pregnancy
test!

Baby is
overdue

Felt baby
move!

Wrote out
birth plan

Heard baby's
heartbeat
Rate:_____

Labor
Day

Thanksgiving

Memorial
Day

Baby
arrived!

Grandparent
visit

Heard baby's
heartbeat
Rate:_____

Organized
the nursery

Morning
sickness

It's a
boy!

Braxton
Hicks

Twins!!!

Heard baby's
heartbeat
Rate:_____

Chose
"going home"
outfits

Checkup

Checkup

Tired all
the time

Wrote out
birth plan

Heard baby's
heartbeat
Rate:_____

Feeling
fabulous

It's a
girl!

Baby came
home

Felt baby
move!

Packed
hospital
overnight bag

Heard baby's
heartbeat
Rate:_____

Glucose
test

Checkup

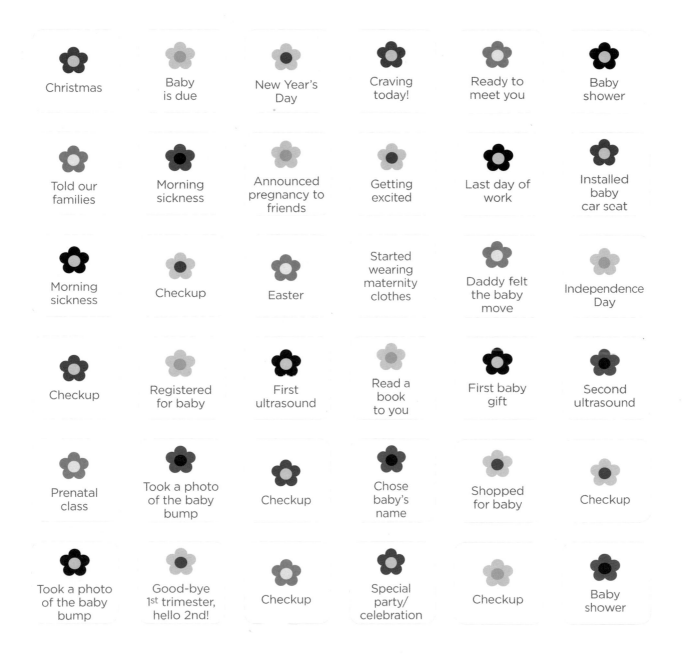

Christmas

Baby is due

New Year's Day

Craving today!

Ready to meet you

Baby shower

Told our families

Morning sickness

Announced pregnancy to friends

Getting excited

Last day of work

Installed baby car seat

Morning sickness

Checkup

Easter

Started wearing maternity clothes

Daddy felt the baby move

Independence Day

Checkup

Registered for baby

First ultrasound

Read a book to you

First baby gift

Second ultrasound

Prenatal class

Took a photo of the baby bump

Checkup

Chose baby's name

Shopped for baby

Checkup

Took a photo of the baby bump

Good-bye 1st trimester, hello 2nd!

Checkup

Special party/ celebration

Checkup

Baby shower